Favorite Poems for Children

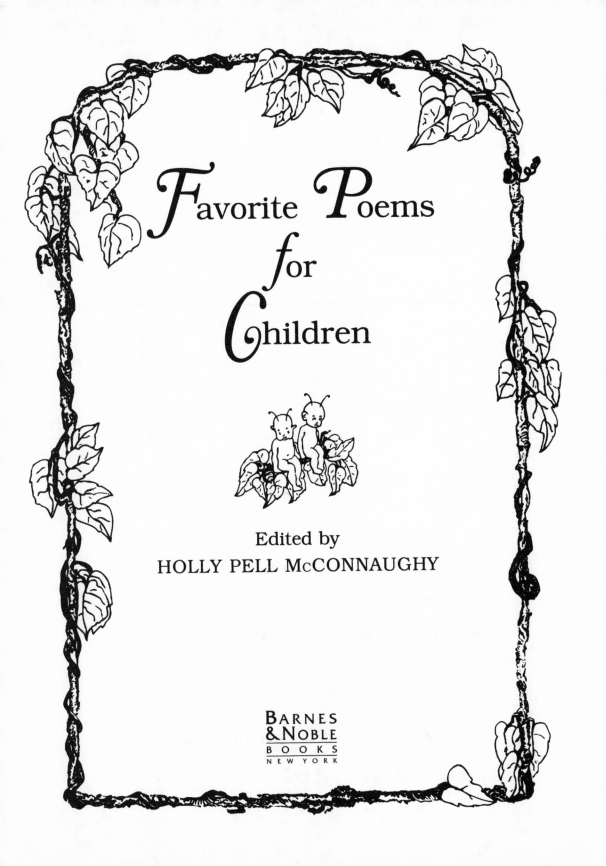

Favorite Poems for Children

Edited by
HOLLY PELL McCONNAUGHY

BARNES
&NOBLE
BOOKS
NEW YORK

This edition published by Barnes & Noble, Inc.

1993 Barnes & Noble Books

ISBN 1-56619-055-X

Printed and bound in the United States of America

01 02 03   M 15 14 13 12 11 10 9

Contents

WIND AND RAIN AND HOLIDAYS

FLOWERS AND FORESTS

FISH, FOWL, AND FUR

MANNERS AND MORALS

CHILDHOOD THOUGHTS AND MERRIMENT

Foreword

I can't remember when I have had so much fun researching a book. The poems that I read ranged from tiny lumps of coal to lovely gems that leaped from the page and caught my imagination with their magic.

I have included quite a few of the old favorites—those poems we all enjoyed as children and now want to pass on to our own families. And there are other poems, also included here, that might not be as readily recognizable but that were simply too enjoyable to pass up.

I hope that you take just as much pleasure in reading this book to yourself and to your children as I did in finding and putting these poems together.

Holly Pell McConnaughy

Silly Sounds and Magical Places

THE MAN IN THE MOON

The Man in the Moon as he sails the sky
Is a very remarkable skipper.
But he made a mistake
When he tried to take
A drink of milk from the Dipper.

He dipped right into the Milky Way
And slowly and carefully filled it.
The Big Bear growled
And the Little Bear howled,
And scared him so he spilled it.

THE LITTLE ELF
by John Kendrick Bangs

I met a little Elf-man, once,
    Down where the lilies blow.
I asked him why he was so small,
    And why he didn't grow.

He slightly frowned, and with his eye
    He looked me through and through.
"I'm quite as big for me," said he,
    "As you are big for you."

I'D LOVE TO BE A FAIRY'S CHILD
by Robert Graves

Children born of fairy stock
Never need for shirt or frock,
Never want for food or fire,
Always get their heart's desire;
Jingle pockets full of gold,
Marry when they're seven years old.
Every fairy child may keep
Two strong ponies and ten sheep;
All have houses, each his own,
Built of brick or granite stone;
They live on cherries, they run wild—
I'd love to be a Fairy's child.

THE DINKEY-BIRD
by Eugene Field

In an ocean, 'way out yonder
    (As all sapient people know),
Is the land of Wonder-Wander,
    Whither children love to go;
It's their playing, romping, swinging,
    That give great joy to me
While the Dinkey-Bird goes singing
    In the amfalula tree!

There the gumdrops grow like cherries
    And taffy's thick as peas—
Caramels you pick like berries
    When, and where, and how you please;
Big red sugar-plums are clinging
    To the cliffs beside that sea
Where the Dinkey-Bird is singing
    In the amfalula tree.

So when children shout and scamper
    And make merry all the day,
When there's naught to put a damper
    To the ardor of their play;
When I hear their laughing ringing,
    Then I'm as sure as sure can be
That the Dinkey-Bird is singing
    In the amfalula tree.

For the Dinkey-Bird's bravuras
　　And staccatos are so sweet—
His roulades, appoggiaturas,
　　And robustos so complete,
That the youth of every nation—
　　Be they near or far away—
Have especial delectation
　　In that gladsome roundelay.

Their eyes grow bright and brighter
　　Their lungs begin to crow,
Their hearts get light and lighter,
　　And their cheeks are all aglow;
For an echo cometh bringing
　　The news to all and me,
That the Dinkey-Bird is singing
　　In the amfalula tree.

I'm sure you like to go there
　　To see your feathered friend—
And so many goodies grow there
　　You would like to comprehend!
Speed, little dreams, you winging
　　To that land across the sea
Where the Dinkey-Bird is singing
　　In the amfalula tree!

THE RIDE TO BUMPVILLE
by Eugene Fields

Play that my knee was a calico mare
    Saddled and bridled for Bumpville;
Leap to the back of this steed,
      if you dare,
    And gallop away to Bumpville!
I hope you'll be sure to sit fast
      in your seat,
For this calico mare is prodigously fleet,
And many adventures you're likely to meet
    As you journey along to Bumpville.

This calico mare both gallops and trots
    While whisking you off to Bumpville;
She paces, she shies, and she stumbles,
      in spots,
    In the tortuous road to Bumpville;
And sometimes this strangely mercurial steed
Will suddenly stop and refuse to proceed,
Which, all will admit, is vexatious indeed,
    When one is en route to Bumpville!

She's scared of the cars when the engine
      goes "Toot!"
    Down by the crossing at Bumpville;
You'd better look out for that
      treacherous brute
    Bearing you off to Bumpville!
With a snort she rears up on her
      hindermost heels,
And executes jigs and Virginia reels—

Words fail to explain how embarrassed
        one feels
    Dancing so wildly to Bumpville!

It's bumpytybump and it's jiggytyjog,
    Journeying on to Bumpville;
It's over the hilltop and down through
        the bog
    You ride on your way to Bumpville;
It's rattletybang over boulder and stump,
There are rivers to ford, there are fences
        to jump;
And the corduroy road it goes bumpytybump,
    Mile after mile to Bumpville!

Perhaps you'll observe it's no easy thing
    Making the journey to Bumpville,
So I think, on the whole, it were prudent
        to bring
    An end to this ride to Bumpville;
For, though she has uttered no protest
        or plaint,
The calico mare must be blowing and faint—
What's more to the point, I'm blowed
        if I ain't!
    So play we have got to Bumpville!

HE THOUGHT HE SAW
by *Lewis Carroll*

He thought he saw a Buffalo
    Upon the chimney-piece:
He looked again, and found it was
    His Sister's Husband's Niece.
"Unless you leave this house," he said,
    "I'll send for the Police!"

He thought he saw a Rattlesnake
    That questioned him in Greek:
He looked again, and found it was
    The Middle of Next Week.
"The one thing I regret," he said,
    "Is that it cannot speak!"

He thought he saw a Banker's Clerk
    Descending from the 'bus:
He looked again, and found it was
    A Hippopotamus.
"If this should stay to dine," he said
    "There won't be much for us!"

He thought he saw a Kangaroo
    That worked a coffee-mill:
He looked again, and found it was
    A Vegetable-Pill.
"Were I to swallow this," he said,
    "I should be very ill!"

He thought he saw a Coach-and-Four
    That stood beside his bed:
He looked again, and found it was
    A Bear without a Head.
"Poor thing," he said, "poor silly thing!
    It's waiting to be fed!"

He thought he saw an Albatross
    That fluttered round the lamp:
He looked again, and found it was
    A Penny-Postage-Stamp.
"You'd best be getting home," he said:
    "The nights are very damp!"

A TRAGIC STORY
by *William Makepeace Thackery*

There lived a sage in days of yore,
And he a handsome pigtail wore;
But wondered much and sorrowed more,
    Because it hung behind him.

He mused upon this curious case,
And swore he'd change the pigtail's place,
And have it hanging at his face,
    Not dangling there behind him.

Says he, "The mystery I've found,—
I'll turn me round,"—he turned him round;
    But still it hung behind him.

Then round and round, and out and in,
All day the puzzled sage did spin;
In vain—it mattered not a pin,—
    The pigtail hung behind him.

And right, and left, and round about,
And up, and down, and in, and out
He turned; but still the pigtail stout
    Hung steadily behind him.

And though his efforts never slack,
And though he twist, and twirl, and tack,
Alas! still faithful to his back,
    The pigtail hangs behind him.

THE WALRUS AND THE CARPENTER
by Lewis Carroll

The sun was shining on the sea,
    Shining with all his might:
He did his very best to make
    The billows smooth and bright—
And this was odd, because it was
    The middle of the night.

The Walrus and the Carpenter
    Were walking close at hand:
They wept like anything to see
    Such quantities of sand:
"If this were only cleared away,"
    They said, "it *would* be grand!"

"If seven maids with seven mops
    Swept it for half a year,
Do you suppose," the Walrus said,
    "That they could get it clear?"
"I doubt it," said the Carpenter,
    And shed a bitter tear.

"O Oysters, come and walk with us!"
    The Walrus did beseech.
"A pleasant talk, a pleasant walk,
    Along the briny beach:
We cannot do with more than four,
    To give a hand to each."

The eldest Oyster looked at him,
    But never a word he said:
The eldest Oyster winked an eye,
    And shook his heavy head—
Meaning to say he did not choose
    To leave the oyster bed.

But four young Oysters hurried up,
    All eager for the treat:
Their coats were brushed, their faces washed,
    Their shoes were clean and neat—
And this was odd, because, you know,
    They hadn't any feet.

Four other Oysters followed them,
    And yet another four;
And thick and fast they came at last,
    And more, and more, and more—
All hopping through the frothy waves,
    And scrambling to the shore.

The Walrus and the Carpenter
    Walked on a mile or so,
And then they rested on a rock
    Conveniently low:
And all the little Oysters stood
    And waited in a row.

"The time has come," the Walrus said,
    "To talk of many things:
Of shoes—and ships—and sealing wax—
    Of cabbages—and kings—
And why the sea is boiling hot—
    And whether pigs have wings."

"But wait a bit," the Oysters cried,
    "Before we have our chat;
For some of us are out of breath,
    And all of us are fat!"
"No hurry!" said the Carpenter.
    They thanked him much for that.

"A loaf of bread," the Walrus said,
    "Is what we chiefly need:
Pepper and vinegar besides
    Are very good indeed—
Now, if you're ready, Oysters dear,
    We can begin to feed."

"But not on us!" the Oysters cried,
    Turning a little blue.
"After such kindness, that would be
    A dismal thing to do!"
"The night is fine," the Walrus said.
    "Do you admire the view?"

"It was so kind of you to come!
    And you are very nice!"
The Carpenter said nothing but
    "Cut us another slice.
I wish you were not quite so deaf—
    I've had to ask you twice!"

"It seems a shame," the Walrus said,
    "To play them such a trick,
After we've brought them out so far,
    And made them trot so quick!"
The Carpenter said nothing but
    "The butter's spread too thick!"

"I weep for you," the Walrus said:
    "I deeply sympathize."
With sobs and tears he sorted out
    Those of the largest size,
Holding his pocket-handkerchief
    Before his streaming eyes.

"O Oysters," said the Carpenter,
    "You've had a pleasant run!
Shall we be trotting home again?"
    But answer came there none—
And this was scarcely odd, because
    They'd eaten every one.

THE WHITING AND THE SNAIL
by Lewis Carroll

"Will you walk a little faster?"
        said a whiting to a snail,
"There's a porpoise close behind us,
        and he's treading on my tail,
See how eagerly the lobsters and the turtles
        all advance!
They are waiting on the shingle—will you come
        and join the dance?
    Will you, won't you, will you, won't you,
        will you join the dance?
    Will you, won't you, will you, won't you,
        won't you join the dance?

"You can really have no notion how delightful
        it will be
When they take us up and throw us,
        with the lobsters, out to sea!"
But the snail replied, "Too far, too far!"
        and gave a look askance—
Said he thanked the whiting kindly,
        but he would not join the dance,
    Would not, could not, would not, could not,
        would not join the dance.
    Would not, could not, would not, could not,
        could not join the dance.

"What matters it how far we go?"
     his scaly friend replied.
"There is another shore, you know,
     upon the other side
The further off from England the nearer
     is to France—
Then turn no pale, beloved snail,
     but come and join the dance.
    Will you, won't you, will you, won't you,
      will you join the dance?
    Will you, won't you, will you, won't you,
      won't you join the dance?

THE SUGAR-PLUM TREE
by Eugene Fields

Have you ever heard of the Sugar-Plum Tree?
    'Tis a marvel of great renown!
It blooms on the shore of the Lollipop sea
    In the garden of Shut-Eye Town;
The fruit that it bears is so wondrously sweet
    (As those who have tasted it say)
That good little children have only to eat
    Of that fruit to be happy next day.

When you've got to the tree, you would have
      a hard time
    To capture the fruit which I sing;
The tree is so tall that no person could climb
    To the boughs where the sugar-plums swing!
But up in that tree sits a chocolate cat,
    And a gingerbread dog prowls below—
And this is the way you contrive to get at
    Those sugar-plums tempting you so:

You say but the word to that gingerbread dog
    And he barks with such terrible zest
That the chocolate cat is at once all agog,
    As her swelling proportions attest.
And the chocolate cat goes cavorting around
    From this leafy limb unto that,
And the sugar-plums tumble, of course,
      to the ground—
    Hurrah for that chocolate cat!

There are marshmallows, gumdrops,
       and peppermint canes,
    With stripings of scarlet and gold,
And you carry away of the treasure that rains
       As much as your apron can hold!
So come, little child, cuddle closer to me
       In your dainty white nightcap and gown
And I'll rock you away to that Sugar-Plum Tree
       In the garden of Shut-Eye Town.

THE LAVENDER BEDS
by William Brighty Rands

The garden was pleasant
      with old-fashioned flowers,
The sunflowers and hollyhocks
      stood up like towers;
There were dark turncap lilies
      and jessamine rare,
And sweet thyme and marjoram
      scented the air.

The moon made the sun-dial
      tell the time wrong;
'Twas too late in the year
      for the nightingale's song;
The box-trees were clipped,
      and the alleys were straight,
Till you came to the shrubbery
      hard by the gate.
The fairies stepped out
      of the lavender beds,
With mob-caps, or wigs, on their quaint
      little heads,
My lord had a sword and my lady a fan;
The music struck up and the dancing began.
I watched them go through with a grave minuet;
Wherever they footed the dew was not wet;
They bowled and they curtsied, the brave
      and the fair;
And laughter like chirping of crickets was there.

Then all of a sudden a church clock
        struck loud:
A flutter, a shiver, was seen in the crowd,
The cock crew, the wind woke, the trees
        tossed their heads,
And the fairy folk hid in the lavender beds.

THE FAIRIES
by William Allingham

Up the airy mountain,
    Down the rushy glen,
We daren't go a-hunting
    For fear of little men;
Wee folk, good folk,
    Trooping all together;
Green jacket, red cap,
    And white owl's feather!

Down along the rocky shore
    Some make their home,
They live on crispy pancakes
    Of yellow tide-foam;
Some in the reeds
    Of the black mountain-lake,
With frogs for their watch-dogs,
    All night awake.

High on the hill-top
    The old King sits;
He is now so old and grey
    He's nigh lost his wits.
With a bridge of white mist
    Columbkill he crosses,
On his stately journeys
    From Slieveleague to Rosses;
Or going up with music
    On cold starry nights,
To sup with the Queen
    Of the gay Northern Lights.

They stole little Bridget
    For seven years long;
When she came down again
    Her friends were all gone.
They took her lightly back,
    Between the night and morrow,
They thought that she was fast asleep,
    But she was dead with sorrow.
They have kept her ever since
    Deep within the lakes,
On a bed of flag-leaves,
    Watching till she wakes.

By the craggy hill-side,
    Through the mosses bare,
They have planted thorn-trees
    For pleasure here and there.
Is any man so daring
    As dig one up in spite,
He shall find their sharpest thorns
    In his bed at night.

Up the airy mountain,
    Down the rushy glen,
We daren't go a-hunting
    For fear of little men;
Wee folk, good folk,
    Trooping all together,
Green jacket, red cap,
    And white owl's feather!

THE TABLE AND THE CHAIR
by Edward Lear

Said the Table to the Chair,
"You can hardly be aware
How I suffer from the heat
And from chilblains on my feet.
If we took a little walk,
We might have a little talk;
Pray let us take the air,"
Said the Table to the Chair.

Said the Chair to the Table,
"Now, you *know* we are not able:
How foolishly you talk,
When you know we *cannot* walk!"
Said the Table with a sigh,
"It can do no harm to try.
I've as many legs as you:
Why can't we walk on two?"

So they both went slowly down,
And walked about the town
With a cheerful bumpy sound
As they toddled round and round;
And everybody cried,
As they hastened to their side,
"See! the Table and the Chair
Have come out to take the air!"

But in going down the alley,
To a castle in a valley,
They completely lost their way,
And wandered all the day;
Till, to see them safely back,
They paid a Ducky-quack,
And a Beetle, and a Mouse,
Who took them to their house.

Then they whispered to each other,
"O delightful little brother,
What a lovely walk we've taken!
Let us dine on beans and bacon."
So the Ducky and the leetle
Browny-Mouse and the Beetle
Dined, and danced upon their heads
Till they toddled to their beds.

WILLIE WINKIE
by *William Miller*

Wee Willie Winkie runs through the town,
Upstairs and doonstairs, in his nicht-gown,
Tirlin' at the window, cryin' at the lock,
"Are the weeans in their bed?—
      for it's noo ten o'clock."

Hey, Willie Winkie! are ye comin' ben?
The cat's singin' gay thrums
      to the sleepin' hen,
The doug's speldered on the floor,
      and disna gie a cheep;
But here's a waukrife laddie,
      that winna fa' asleep.

Onything but sleep, ye rogue!—
      glowerin' like the moon.
Rattlin' in an airn jug wi' an airn spoon,
Rumblin', tumblin' roun' about,
      crawin' like a cock,
Skirlin' like a kenna-what—
      wauknin' sleepin' folk!

Hey, Willie Winkie! the wean's in a creel!
Waumblin' aff a bodie's knee like a vera eel,
Ruggin' at the cat's lug,
      and ravellin' a' her thrums:
Hey, Willie Winkie!—
      See, there he comes!

CALICO PIE
by *Edward Lear*

Calico Pie,
The little birds fly
Down to the calico-tree:
Their wings were blue,
And they sang "tilly-loo!"
Till away they flew;
And they never came back,
They never came back,
They never came back,
They never came back to me!

Calico jam,
The little Fish swam
Over the Syllabub Sea.
He took off his hat
To the Sole and the Sprat,
And the Willeby-wat:
But he never came back to me;
He never came back,
He never came back,
He never came back to me.

Calico ban,
The little Mice ran
To be ready in time for tea;
Flippity flup,
They drank it all up,
And danced in the cup:
But they never came back to me;
They never came back,
They never came back,
They never came back to me.

Calico drum,
The Grasshoppers come,
The Butterfly, Beetle, and Bee,
Over the ground,
Around and round,
With a hop and a bound;
But they never came back,
They never came back,
They never came back,
They never came back to me.

JABBERWOCKY
by *Lewis Carroll*

"Twas brillig, and the slithy toves
    Did gyre and gimble in the wabe;
All mimsy were the borogroves,
    And the mome raths outgrabe.

"Beware the Jabberwock, my son!
    The jaws that bite, the claws that catch!
Beware the Jubjub bird, and shun
    The frumtious Bandersnatch!"

He took his vorpal sword in hand:
    Long time the manxome foe he sought.—
So rested he by the Tumtum tree,
    And stood awhile in thought.

And as in uffish thought he stood,
    The Jabberwock, with eyes of flame,
Came whiffling through the tulgey wood,
    And burbled as it came!

One, two! One, two! And through and through
    The vorpal blade went snicker-snack!
He left it dead, and with its head
    He went galumphing back.

"And hast thou slain the Jabberwock?
    Come to my arms, my beamish boy!
O frabjous day! Callooh! Callay!
    He chortled in his joy.

"Twas brillig, and the slithy toves
    Did gyre and gimble in the wabe;
All mimsy were the borogroves,
    And the mome raths outgrabe.

FIVE NONSENSE VERSES
by Edward Lear

There was an Old Man with a beard,
Who said, "It is just as I feared!
    Two Owls and a Hen,
    Four Larks and a Wren,
Have all built their nests in my beard!

There was an Old Man in a tree,
Who was horribly bored by a bee;
    When they said "Does it buzz?"
    He replied, "Yes, it does!
It's a regular brute of a bee!"

There was an Old Man in a boat,
Who said, "I'm afloat! I'm afloat!"
    When they said, "No, you ain't!"
    He was ready to faint,
That unhappy old man in a boat.

There was an Old Man with a poker,
Who painted his face with red ochre;
    When they said, "You're a Guy!"
    He made no reply,
But knocked them all down with his poker.

There was an Old Man who said, "Hush!"
I perceive a young bird in this bush!"
    When they said, "Is it small?"
    He replied, "Not at all!
It is four times as big as the bush!"

The Reverend Henry Ward Beecher
Called a hen a most elegant creature.
    The hen, pleased with that,
    Laid an egg in his hat,—
And thus did the hen reward Beecher.

WYNKEN, BLYNKEN, AND NOD
by Eugene Fields

Wynken, Blynken, and Nod one night
Sailed off in a wooden shoe—
Sailed on a river of crystal light,
Into a sea of dew.
"Where are you going, and what do you wish?"
The old moon asked the three.
"We have come to fish for the herring fish
That live in this beautiful sea;
Nets of silver and gold have we!"
      Said Wynken,
      Blynken,
      And Nod.

The old moon laughed and sang a song
As they rocked in the wooden shoe,
And the wind that sped them all night long
Ruffled the waves of dew.
The little stars were the herring fish
That lived in that beautiful sea—
"Now cast your nets wherever you wish—
Never afeard are we";
So cried the stars to the fishermen three:
      Wynken,
      Blynken,
      And Nod.

All night long their nets they threw
To the stars in the twinkling foam—
Then down from the skies came the wooden shoe,
Bringing the fishermen home;
'Twas all so pretty a sail it seemed
As if it could not be,
And some folks thought 'twas a dream they'd
       dreamed
Of sailing that beautiful sea—
But I shall name you the fishermen three:
      Wynken,
      Blynken,
      And Nod.

Wynken and Blynken are two little eyes,
And Nod is a little head,
And the wooden shoe that sailed the skies
Is a wee one's trundle-bed.
So shut your eyes while mother sings
Of wonderful sights that be,
And you shall see the beautiful things
As you rock in the misty sea,
Where the old shoe rocked the fishermen three:
      Wynken,
      Blynken,
      And Nod.

THE OWL AND THE PUSSY-CAT
by Edward Lear

The Owl and the Pussy-cat went to sea
 In a beautiful pea-green boat:
They took some honey, and plenty of money
 Wrapped up in a five pound note.
The Owl looked up to the stars above,
 And sang to a small guitar,
"O lovely Pussy, O Pussy, my love,
 What a beautiful Pussy you are,
 What a beautiful Pussy you are,
   You are,
   You are,
 What a beautiful Pussy you are!"

Pussy said to the Owl, "You elegant fowl,
 How charmingly sweet you sing!
Oh! let us be married; too long we have tarried;
 But what shall we do for a ring?"
They sailed away, for a year and a day,
 To the land where the bong-tree grows;
And there in a wood a Piggy-wig stood,
 With a ring at the end of his nose,
   His nose,
   His nose,
 With a ring at the end of his nose.

"Dear Pig, are you willing to sell for one shilling
　　Your ring?" Said the Piggy, "I will."
So they took it away, and were married next day
　　By the Turkey who lives on the hill.
They dined on mince and slices of quince,
　　Which they ate with a runcible spoon;
And hand in hand, on the edge of the sand,
　　They danced by the light of the moon,
　　　　The moon,
　　　　The moon,
They danced by the light of the moon.

In the Nursery

GOOD NIGHT!

Little baby, lay your head
On your pretty cradle-bed;
Shut your eye-peeps, now the day
And the light are gone away;
All the clothes are tucked in tight;
Little baby dear, good night.

LOOKING FORWARD
by Robert Louis Stevenson

When I am grown to men's estate
I shall be very proud and great.
And tell the other girls and boys
Not to meddle with my toys.

SLEEPY HARRY

Get up, little boy, you are sleeping too long,
Your brother is dressed and singing a song,
And you must be wakened,—oh! fie!

Come, come open the curtains,
    and let in the light,
For children should only be sleepy at night,
When the stars may be seen in the sky.

THERE WAS A MONKEY

There was a monkey climbed up a tree,
When he fell down, then down fell he.

There was a crow sat on a stone,
When he was gone, then there was none.

There was an old wife did eat an apple,
When she had ate two, she had ate a couple.

There was a horse going to the mill,
When he went on, he stood not still.

There was a butcher cut his thumb,
When it did bleed, then blood did come.

There was a lackey ran a race,
When he ran fast, he ran apace.

There was a cobbler clouting shoon,
When they were mended, they were done.

There was a chandler making a candle,
When he them strip, he did them handle.

There was a navy went into Spain,
When it returned, it came again.

CACKLE, CACKLE, MOTHER GOOSE!

Cackle, cackle, Mother Goose!
Have you any feathers loose?
Truly have I, pretty fellow,
Half enough to fill a pillow;
And here are quills, take one or two,
And down to make a bed for you.

THE NUT TREE

I had a little nut tree,
    Nothing would it bear
But a silver nutmeg
    And a golden pear;
The King of Spain's daughter
    She came to see me,
And all because of my little nut-tree.
I skipped over the water,
    I danced over the sea,
And all the birds in the air couldn't catch me.

THE QUEEN OF HEARTS

The Queen of Hearts
She made some tarts,
All on a summer's day;
The Knave of Hearts
He stole those tarts,
And with them ran away.

The King of Hearts
Called for the tarts,
And beat the Knave full sore;
The Knave of Hearts
Brought back the tarts,
And vowed he'd steal no more.

SHOWING HOW THE CAVERN FOLLOWED THE HUT'S ADVICE
by John Hookham Frere

This fable is a very short one:
The cave resolved to make his fortune;
He got a door and in a year
Enriched himself with wine and beer.

Mamma will ask you, can you tell her,
What did the cave become?—A cellar.

I'M GLAD

I'm glad the sky is painted blue,
    And the earth is painted green,
WIth such a lot of nice fresh air
    All sandwiched in between.

HI! DIDDLE DIDDLE

    Hi! diddle diddle,
    The cat and the fiddle,
The cow jumped over the moon;
    The little dog laughed
    To see such sport,
While the dish ran after the spoon.

POOR COCK ROBIN

Who killed Cock Robin?
   I, said the Sparrow,
   With my bow and arrow,
I killed Cock Robin.

Who saw him die?
   I, said the Magpie,
   With my little eye,
I saw him die.

Who caught his blood?
   I, said the Fish,
   With my little dish,
I caught his blood.

Who made his shroud?
   I, said the Eagle,
   With my thread and needle,
I made his shroud.

Who'll dig his grave?
   The Owl, with aid
   Of mattock and spade
Will dig Robin's grave.

Who'll be the parson?
   I, said the Rook,
   With my little book,
I'll be the parson.

Who'll be the clerk?
    I, said the Lark,
    If not in the dark,
I'll be the clerk.

Who'll carry him to the grave?
    I, said the Kite,
    If not in the night,
I'll carry him to his grave.

Who'll be the chief mourner?
    I, said the Swan,
    I'm sorry he's gone,
I'll be chief mourner.

Who'll bear his pall?
    We, said the Wren,
    Both the cock and hen,
We'll bear his pall.

Who'll toll the bell?
    I, said the Bull,
    Because I can pull,
And I'll pull the bell.

Who'll lead the way?
    I, said the Martin,
    When ready for starting,
And I'll lead the way.

All the birds in the air
    Began sighing and sobbing,
When they heard the bell toll
    For poor Cock Robin.

To all it concerns,
    This notice apprises,
The sparrow's for trial
    At next bird assizes.

SEE, SAW, MARGERY DAW

See, saw, Margery Daw,
    Baby shall have a new master.
She can earn but a penny a day,
    Because she can't work any faster.

See, saw, Margery Daw,
    Sold her bed to lie upon straw.
Was not she a naughty puss,
    To sell her bed to lie on a truss?

OH! DEAR!

Oh! dear! what can the matter be?
Dear! dear! what can the matter be?
Oh! dear! what can the matter be?
Johnny's so long at the fair.

He promis'd he'd buy me a fairing should please
       me,
And then for a kiss, oh! he vow'd he would tease
       me;
He promis'd he'd bring me a bunch of blue rib-
       bons
To tie up my bonny brown hair.

Oh! dear! what can the matter be?
Dear! dear! what can the matter be?
Oh! dear! what can the matter be?
Johnny's so long at the fair.

He promis'd he'd bring me a basket of posies,
A garland of lilies, a garland of roses,
A little straw hat, to set off the blue ribbons
That tie up my bonny brown hair.

OLD KING COLE

Old King Cole
Was a merry old soul,
And a merry old soul was he;
He called for his pipe,
And he called for his bowl,
And he called for his fiddlers three.
Every fiddler, he had a fiddle,
And a very fine fiddle had he;
Twe tweedle doo, tweedle doo,
Went the fiddlers.
Oh, there's none so rare,
As can compare
With King Cole and his fiddlers three!

THE MAN IN THE WILDERNESS

The man in the wilderness asked me,
How many strawberries grew in the sea?
I answered him as I thought good,
As many red herrings as grew in the wood.

UPON A BLACK HORSE-ILY

Upon a black horse-ily
A man came riding cross-ily;
A lady out did come-ily,
Said she, "No one's at home-ily,

"But only little people-y,
Who've gone to bed to sleep-ily."
The rider on his horse-ily
Said to the lady, cross-ily,

"But are they bad or good-ily?
I want it understood-ily."
"Oh they act bad and bold-ily,
And don't do what their told-ily."

"Good-by!" said he, "dear Ma'am-ily,
I've nothing for your family."
And scampered off like mouse-ily
Away, way from the house-ily.

BA, BA, BLACK SHEEP

Ba, ba, black sheep,
    Have you any wool?
Yes sir, no sir,
    Three bags full.
One for my master,
    And one for my dame,
But none for the little boy
    Who cries in the lane.

COCK A DOODLE DOO!

Cock a doodle doo!
My dame has lost her shoe;
My master's lost his fiddling stick,
And don't know what to do.

Cock a doodle doo!
What is my dame to do?
Till master finds his fiddling stick,
She'll dance without her shoe.

Cock a doodle doo!
My dame has found her shoe,
And master's found his fiddling stick,
Sing doodle doodle do!

Cock a doodle doo!
My dame will dance with you,
While master fiddles his fiddling stick,
For dame and doodle doo.

PUSSY'S IN THE WELL

Ding, dong, bell,
Pussy's in the well!
Who put her in?
Little Tommy Lin.
Who pulled her out?
Dog with a snout.
What a naughty boy was that
To drown poor pussy-cat,
Who never did any harm,
But kill's the mice in his master's barn.

GOOSEY, GOOSEY GANDER

Goosey, goosey gander,
    Whither shall I wander?
Up stairs, down stairs,
    And in my lady's chamber:
There I met an old man
    That would not say his prayers,
I took him by the left leg,
    And threw him down the stairs.

TOM THUMB'S ALPHABET

A was an archer, who shot at a frog;
B was a butcher, he had a great dog;
C was a captain, all covered with lace;
D was a drunkard, and had a red face;
E was an esquire, with pride on his brow;
F was a farmer, and followed the plough;
G was a gamester, who had but ill luck;
I was an innkeeper, who loved to bouse;
J was a joiner, and built up a house;
K is King Edward, who governs England;
L was a lady, who had a white hand;
M was a miser, and hoarded up gold;
N was a nobleman, gallant and bold;
O was an oyster girl, and went about town;
P was a parson, and wore a black gown;
Q was a queen, who wore a silk slip;
R was a robber, who wanted a whip;
S was a sailor; and spent all he got;
T was a tinker, and mended a pot;
U was an usurer, a miserable elf;
V was a vintner, who drank all himself;
W was a watchman, and guarded the door;
X was expensive, and so became poor;
Y was a youth, that did not love school;
Z was a zany, a poor harmless fool.

MATHEMATICS

Multiplication is vexation
  Division is as bad;
The Rule of Three perplexes me
  And Practice drives me mad.

AT THE SEASIDE
by Robert Louis Stevenson

When I was down beside the sea
A wooden spade they gave to me
  To dig the sandy shore.

My holes were empty like a cup,
In every hole the sea came up,
  Till it could come no more.

A LITTLE HOBBY-HORSE
by Eliza Grove

There was a little hobby-horse,
    Whose name I do not know,—
An idle little hobby-horse,
    That said he wouldn't go.

But his master said, "If it be so
    That you will only play,
You idle rogue, you shall not eat
    My nice sweet clover-hay!"

Then Hobby shook his saucy head,
    And said, "If that's the case,
Rather than go without my hay,
    I'll try and mend my pace."

A LITTLE BIRD

Once I saw a little bird
    Come hop, hop, hop;
So I cried, "Little bird,
    Will you stop, stop, stop?"
And was going to window
    To say, "How do you do?"
But he shook his little tail
    And far away he flew.

SINGING

by Robert Louis Stevenson

Of speckled eggs the birdie sings—
　　And nests among the trees;
The sailor sings of ropes and things
　　In ships upon the seas.

The children sing in far Japan,
　　The children sing in Spain;
The organ with the organ man
　　Is singing in the rain.

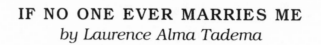

IF NO ONE EVER MARRIES ME
by *Laurence Alma Tadema*

If no one ever marries me
    I shan't mind very much;
I shall buy a squirrel in a cage
    And a little rabbit-hutch:

I shall have a cottage near a wood,
    And a pony all my own,
And a little lamb quite clean and tame
    That I can take to town:

And when I'm getting really old,
    —At twenty-eight or nine—
I shall buy a little orphan-girl
    And bring her up as mine.

NURSERY RHYME

I had a little hobby horse
    His name was Tommy Gray,
His head was made of peas straw,
    His body made of hay;
I saddled him and bridled him,
    And rode him up to town,
There came a little puff of wind
    And blew him up and down.

THE CROCODILE

How doth the little crocodile
    Improve his shining tail,
And pour the waters of the Nile
    On every golden scale!

How cheerfully he seems to grin
    How neatly spreads his claws,
And welcomes little fishes in
    With gently smiling jaws.

WHISKY FRISKY

Whisky Frisky
Hippity Hop,
Up he goes
To the tree top!

Whirly, Twirly,
Round and round,
Down he scampers
To the ground.

Furly Curly
What a tail!
Tall as a feather
Broad as a sail!

Where's his supper?
In the shell,
Snappy, cracky,
Out it fell!

RIDDLES

There was a girl in our town,
Silk an' satin was her gown,
Silk an' satin, gold an' velvet,
Guess her name, three times I've telled it.
(Ann)

As soft as silk, as white as milk,
As bitter as gall, a thick green wall,
And a brown coat covers me all.
(A walnut)

In marble walls as white as milk,
Lined with a skin as soft as silk;
Without a fountain crystal clear,
A golden apple doth appear.
No doors there are to this stronghold,
Yet thieves break in and steal the gold.
(An egg)

Thirty white horses upon a red hill,
Now they tramp, now they champ, now they stand
still.
(Teeth)

Old Mother Twitchett had but one eye,
And a long tail which she let fly;
And every time she went over a gap,
She left a bit of her tail in a trap.
(A needle and thread)

As I went through a garden gap,
Who should I meet but Dick Red-Cap!
A stick in his hand, a stone in his throat,
If you'll tell me this riddle,
        I'll give you a groat.

                    (A cherry)

Little Nanny Etticoat,
In a white petticoat,
And a red nose;
The longer she stands
The shorter she grows.
            (A candle)

Wind and Rain and Holidays

THE MONTHS
by Sara Coleridge

January brings the snow,
Makes our feet and fingers glow.

February brings the rain,
Thaws the frozen lake again.

March brings breezes sharp and chill,
Shakes the dancing daffodil.

April brings the primrose sweet,
Scatters daisies at our feet.

May brings flocks of pretty lambs,
Sporting round their fleecy dams.

June brings tulips, lilies, roses,
Fills the children's hands with posies.

Hot July brings thunder-showers,
Apricots, and gilly-flowers.

August brings the sheaves of corn;
Then the harvest home is borne.

Warm September brings the fruit;
Sportsmen then begin to shoot.

Brown October brings the pheasant,
Then to gather nuts is pleasant.

Dull November brings the blast—
Hark! the leaves are whirling fast.

Cold December brings the sleet,
Blazing fire, and Christmas treat.

THE RAIN

The rain came down in torrents
    And Mary said, "Oh! dear,
I'll have to wear my water proof,
    And rubbers too, I fear."
So carefully protected—she started
       off to school
    When the big round sun
Came out and chuckled—"April Fool."

WIND SONG

Here comes the wind, with a noise and a whirr,
Out on the streets he is making a stir.
Now he sends flying a fine, stiff hat,
Tosses and leaves it all muddy and flat;
Turns an umbrella quite inside out,
Tears up stray papers and scatters about,
Makes big balloons out of ladies' long capes,
Skirts into sails, then—the queerest of shapes.
The wind is an enemy, often we say:
"We never quite like it—a windy day!"

The wind blows the seeds from their close
        little pods
And scatters them far away—rods upon rods;
He plants them where never an eye could see
Place for their growing and blooming to be.
He blows away rain, and scatters the dew,
He sweeps the earth clean and makes it
        all new.
He blows away sickness and brings good health
He comes overladen with beauty and wealth.
Oh, the wind is a friend! Let us always say:
"We love it! We love it!—a windy day!"

EASTER EGGS

Humpty Dumpty has country cousins
Who come to the city in Spring by dozens;
They make such a brilliant show in town
You'd think that a rainbow had tumbled down.
Blue and yellow and pink and green,
The gayest gowns that ever were seen.
Purple and gold and oh! such style;
They are all the rage for a little while
But their visit is short for no one stays
After the Easter holidays.

A WEATHER RULE

If the evening's red and the morning gray,
It is the sign of a bonny day;
If the evening's gray and the morning's red,
The lamb and the ewe will go wet to bed.

WHICH WAY DOES THE WIND BLOW?
by Nancy Aikin

Which way does the wind blow,
    Which way does he go?
He rides over the water,
    He rides over the snow;

O'er wood and o'er valley,
    And o'er rocky height,
Which the goat cannot traverse,
    He taketh his flight.

He rages and tosses
    In every bare tree,
As, if you look upwards,
    You plainly may see.

But whence he both cometh
    And whither he goes,
There's never a scholar
    In England who knows.

OXFORDSHIRE CHILDREN'S MAY SONG

Spring is coming, spring is coming,
　　Birdies, build your nest;
Weave together straw and feather,
　　Doing each your best.

Spring is coming, spring is coming,
　　Flowers are coming too:
Pansies, lilies, daffodillies,
　　Now are coming through.

Spring is coming, spring is coming,
　　All around is fair;
Shimmer and quiver on the river,
　　Joy is everywhere.

We wish you a happy May.

THE WIND

by Robert Louis Stevenson

I say you toss the kites on high
And blow the birds about the sky;
And all around I heard you pass,
Like ladies' skirts across the grass—
    O wind, a-blowing all day long,
    O wind, that sings so loud a song!

I saw the different things you did,
But always you yourself you hid.
I felt you push, I heard you call,
I could not see yourself at all—
    O wind, a'blowing all day long,
    O wind, that sings so loud a song!

O you that are so strong and cold,
O blower, are you young or old?
Are you a beast of field and tree,
Or just stronger child than me?
    O wind, a-blowing all day long,
    O wind, that sings so loud a song!

LITTLE RAIN-DROPS
by Ann Hawkshawe

Oh! where do you come from
    You little drops of rain;
Pitter patter, pitter patter
    Down the window-pane?

They won't let me walk,
    And they won't let me play,
And they won't let me go
    Out of doors at all to-day.

They put away my playthings
    Because I broke them all,
And they locked up all my bricks,
    And took away my ball.

Tell me, little rain drops,
    Is that the way you play,
Pitter patter, pitter patter,
    All the rainy day?

They say I'm very naughty,
    But I've nothing else to do
But sit here at the window;
    I should like to play with you.

The little rain-drops cannot speak,
    But "pitter, patter, pat"
Means, "We can play on this side,
    Why can't you play on that?"

THE RAIN

"Open the window, and let me in,"
    Sputters the merry rain;
"I want to splash down on the carpet, dear,
    And I can't get through the pane.

"Here I've been tapping outside to you,
    Why don't you come, if you're there?
The windows are shut or I'd dash right in,
    And stream down the attic stair.

"I've washed the windows, I've spattered the
       blinds,
    And that is not half what I have done;
I've bounced on the step and the sidewalk too
    Till I've made the good people run.

BED IN SUMMER
by Robert Louis Stevenson

In winter I get up at night
And dress by yellow candle-light.
In summer, quite the other way,
I have to go to bed by day.

I have to go to bed and see
The birds still hopping on the tree,
Or hear the grown-up people's feet
Still going past me in the street.

And does it not seem hard to you
When all the sky is clear and blue,
And I should like so much to play,
To have to go to bed by day?

I WANDERED SO LONELY AS A CLOUD
by *William Wordsworth*

I wandered so lonely as a cloud
    That floats on high o'er vales and hills,
When all at once I saw a crowd,
    A host of golden daffodils:
Beside the lake, beneath the trees,
Fluttering and dancing in the breeze.

Continuous as the stars that shine
    And twinkle on the milky way,
They stretched in never-ending line
    Along the margin of the bay:
Then thousand saw I at a glance,
Tossing their heads in sprightly dance.

The waves beside them danced, but they
    Out-did the sparkling waves in glee:—
A poet could not but be gay,
    In such a jocund company;
I gazed—and gazed—but little thought
What wealth the show to me had brought.

For oft, when on my couch I lie
    In vacant or in pensive mood,
They flash upon that inward eye
    Which is the bliss of solitude;
And then my heart with pleasure fills,
And dances with the daffodils.

HOW THE KITE LEARNED TO FLY

"I never can do it," the little kite said,
As he looked at the others high over his head;
"I know I should fall if I tried to fly."
"Try," said the big kite; "only try,
Or I fear you never will learn at all."
But the little kite said, "I'm afraid I'll fall."

The big kite nodded: "Ah, well, good-by;
I'm off"; and he rose toward the tranquil sky.
Then the little kite's paper stirred at the sight,
And trembling he shook himself free for flight.
First whirling and frightened, then braver grown,
Up, up he rose through the air alone,
Till the big kite looking down could see
The little one rising steadily.

Then how the little kite thrilled with pride,
As he sailed with the big kite side by side!
While far below he could see the ground,
And the boys like small spots moving round.
They rested high in the quiet air,
And only the birds and clouds were there.
"Oh, how happy I am!" the little kite cried,
"And all because I was brave and tried."

WHO HAS SEEN THE WIND
by Christina Georgina Rossetti

Who has seen the wind?
　　Neither I nor you:
But when the leaves hang trembling,
　　The wind is passing through.

Who has seen the wind?
　　Neither you nor I:
But when the trees bow down their heads,
　　The wind is passing by.

OCTOBER'S PARTY
by George Cooper

October gave a party;
    The leaves by hundreds came—
The Chestnuts, Oaks and Maples,
    And leaves of every name.
The Sunshine spread a carpet,
    And everything was grand,
Miss Weather led the dancing,
    Professor Wind the band.

The Chestnuts came in yellow,
    The Oaks in crimson dressed;
The lovely Misses Maple
    In scarlet looked their best;
All balanced to their partners,
    And gaily fluttered by;
The sight was like a rainbow
    New fallen from the sky.

Then, in the rustic hollow,
    At hide-and-seek they played,
The party closed at sundown,
    And everybody stayed.
Professor Wind played louder;
    They flew along the ground;
And then the party ended
    In jolly "hands around."

COME, LITTLE LEAVES
by George Cooper

"Come, little leaves," said the wind one day.
"Come over the meadows with me and play;
Put on your dresses of red and gold,
For summer is gone and the days grow cold."

Soon as the leaves heard the wind's loud call,
Down they came fluttering, one and all;
Over the brown fields they danced and flew,
Singing the sweet little song they knew.

"Cricket, good-by, we've been friends so long,
Little brook, sing us your farewell song;
Say you are sorry to see us go;
Ah, you will miss us, right well we know.

"Dear little lambs in your fleecy fold,
Mother will keep you from harm and cold;
Fondly we watched you in vale and glade,
Say, will you dream of our loving shade?"

Dancing and whirling, the little leaves went,
Winter had called them, and they were content;
Soon, fast asleep in their earthy beds,
The snow laid a coverlid over their heads.

WHEN THE FROST IS ON THE PUNKIN
by James Whitcomb Riley

When the frost is on the punkin and
    the fodder's in the shock,
And you hear the kyouck and gobble
    of the struttin' turkey-cock,
And the clackin' of the guineys, and
    the cluckin' of the hens,
And the rooster's hallylooyer as he
    tiptoes on the fence;
O, it's then's the times a feller is
    a-feelin' at his best,
With the risin' sun to greet him from
    a night of peaceful rest,
As he leaves the house, bareheaded,
    and goes out to feed the stock,
When the frost is on the punkin and
    the fodder's in the chock.

They's something kindo' harty-like
    about the atmusfere
When the heat of summer's over and
    the coolin' fall is here—
Of course we miss the flowers, and the
    blossoms on the trees,
And the mumble of the hummin'-birds
    and buzzin' of the bees;

But the air's so appetizin'; and the
　　landscape through the haze
Of as crisp and sunny morning of the
　　eirly autumn days
Is a pictur' that no painter has the
　　colorin' to mock—
When the frost is on the punkin and
　　the fodder's in the shock.

The husky, rusty russel of the tossels
　　of the corn,
And the raspin' of the tangled leaves,
　　as golden as the morn;
The stubble in the furries—kindo'
　　lonesome-like, but still
A-preaching' sermuns to us of the
　　barns they growed to fill;
The strawstack in the medder, and the
　　reaper in the shed;
The hosses in theyr stalls below—the
　　clover overhead!—
O, it sets my hart a-clickin' like the
　　tickin' of a clock,
When the frost is on the punkin and
　　the fodder's in the shock.

Then your apples all is gethered, and
    the ons a feller keeps
Is poured around the cellar-floor in
    red and yeller heaps;
And you cider-makin' 's over, and
    your wimmen-folks is through
With their mince and apple-butter,
    and theyr souse and saussage, too!
I don't know how to tell it—but ef
    sich thing could be
As the Angels wantin' boardin', and
    they'd call around on me—
I'd want to 'commodate 'em—all the
    whole indurin' flock—
When the frost is on the punkin and
    the fodder's in the shock!

THANKSGIVING DAY
by Lydia Maria Child

Over the river and through the wood,
   To grandfather's house we go;
      The horse knows the way
      To carry the sleigh
Through the white and drifted snow.

Over the river and through the wood—
   Oh, how the wind does blow!
      It stings the toes
      And bites the nose,
As over the ground we go.

Over the river and through the wood,
   To have a first-rate play.
      Hear the bells ring,
      "Ting-a-ling-ding!"
Hurrah for Thanksgiving Day!

Over the river and through the wood
   Trot fast, my dapple-gray!
      Spring over the ground,
      Like a hunting-hound!
For this is Thanksgiving Day.

Over the river and through the wood,
　　And straight through the barnyard gate.
　　　　We seem to go
　　　　Extremely slow,—
　　It is so hard to wait!

Over the river and through the wood—
　　Now grandmother's cap I spy!
　　　　Hurrah for the fun!
　　　　Is the pudding done?
　　Hurrah for the pumpkin pie!

JACK FROST

Jack Frost rapped on the window-pane
    And knocked on the door with his icicle cane.
"Excuse me," I said. "The door is shut tight,
    I'd rather you did not come in to-night."
So he wrote his name all over the glass
    And the baby sneezed as she heard him pass.

SNOWMAN

One day we built a snowman
    We made him out of snow.
You'd ought to see how fine he was
    All white from head to toe.
We poured some water on him
    And froze him—legs and ears,
And when we went indoors to bed,
    I said he'd last two years.
But in the night, a warmer kind
    Of wind began to blow
And Winter cried and ran away,
    And with it ran the snow.
And in the morning when we went,
    To bid our friend, "Good day,"
There wasn't any snowman there,
    He'd melted all away.

OLD WINTER
by Thomas Noel

Old Winter sad, in snowy clad,
  Is making a doleful din;
But let him howl till he crack his jowl,
  We will not let him in.

Ay, let him lift from the billowy drift
  His hoary, haggard form,
And scowling stand, with his wrinkled hand
  Outstretching to the storm.

And let his weird and sleety beard
  Stream loose upon the blast,
And, rustling, chime to the tinkling rime
  From his bald head falling fast.

Let his baleful breath shed blight and death
  On herb and flower and tree;
And brooks and ponds in crystal bonds
  Bind fast, but what care we?

Let him push at the door—in the chimney roar,
  And rattle the window pane;
Let him in at us spy with his icicle eye,
  But he shall not entrance gain.

Let him gnaw, forsooth, with his freezing tooth,
    On our roof tiles, till he tire;
But we care not a whit, as we jovial sit
    Before our blazing fire.

Come lads, let's sing, till the rafters ring;
    Some, push the can about;—
From our snug fire-side this Chrismas-tide
    We'll keep old Winter out.

SNOW-FLAKES
by Mary Mapes Dodge

Whenever a snow-flake leaves the sky,
It turns and turns to say "Good-bye!
Good-bye, dear cloud, so cool and gray!"
Then lightly travels on its way.

And when a snow-flake finds a tree,
"Good-day!" it says—'Good-day to thee!
Thou art so bare and lonely, dear,
I'll rest and call my comrades here."

But when a snow-flake, brave and meek,
Lights on a rosy maiden's cheek,
It starts—"How warm and soft the day!
'Tis summer!"—and it melts away.

ONCE THERE WAS A SNOWMAN

Once there was a snowman
    Stood outside the door
Thought he'd like to come inside
    And run around the floor;
Thought he'd like to warm himself
    By the fire light red;
Thought he'd like to climb up
    On the big white bed.
So he called the North Wind, "Help me now I pray.
    I'm completely frozen, standing here all day."
So the North Wind came along and blew him in
        the door,
    And now there's nothing left of him
But a puddle on the floor.

JEST 'FORE CHRISTMAS
by Eugene Field

Father calls me William, sister calls me Will,
Mother calls me Willie, but fellers
    call me Bill!
Mighty glad I ain't a girl—ruther be a boy,
Without them sashes, curls, an' things
    that's worn by Fauntleroy!
Love to chawnk green apples an' go swimmin'
    in the lake—
Hate to take the castor-ile they give
    for belly-ache!
'Most all the time, the whole year round,
    there ain't no flies on me,
But jest 'fore Christmas I'm as good
    as I kin be!

Got a yeller dog named Sport, sick him
    on the cat;
First thing she knows she doesn't know
    where she is at!
Got a clipper sled, an' when us kids goes out
    to slide,
'Long comes the grocery cart, an' we all hook
    a ride!

But sometimes when the grocery man is worried
    an' cross,
He reaches at us with his whip, an' larrups up
    his hoss,
An' then I laff an' holler, "Oh, ye never
    teched *me!*"
But jest 'fore Christmas I'm as good
    as I can be!

Gran'ma says she hopes that when I git
    to be a man,
I'll be a missionarer like her oldest brother,
    Dan,
As was et up by the cannibuls that lives
    in Ceylon Isle,
Where every prospeck pleases, an' only man
    is vile!
But gran'ma she has never been to see
    a Wild West show,
Nor read the life of Daniel Boone, or else
    I guess she'd know
That Buff'lo Bill an' cowboys is good enough
    for me!
Excep' jest 'fore Christmas, when I'm as good
    as I kin be!

And then Old Sport he hangs around, so solemn-
    like an' still
His eyes they keep a-sayin': "What's the matter,
    little Bill?"

The old cat sneaks down off her perch an' won-
    ders what's become
Of them two enemies of hern that used to make
    things hum!
But I am so perlite an' 'tend so earnestly
    to biz,
That mother says to father: "How improved
    our Willie is!"
But father, havin' been a boy hisself,
    suspicions me
When, jest 'fore Christmas, I'm as good
    as I kin be!

For Christmas, with its lots an' lots of candies,
    cakes, an' toys,
Was made, they say, for proper kids an' not
    for naughty boys;
So wash yer face an' bresh yer hair, an' mind yer
    p's and q's,
An' don't bust out yer pantaloons, an' don't wear
    out yer shoes;
Say "Yessum" to the ladies, an' "Yessur"
    to the men,
An' when they's company, don't pass yer plate
    for pie again;
But, thinkin' of the things yer'd like to see
    upon that tree,
Jest 'fore Christmas be as good as yer kin be!

MY DOLLY AND HER STOCKING

My dolly hung her stocking up,
    And Santa filled it full,
There were some nuts and sugar-plums
    And a pretty dress of wool—
The sweetest lace-trimmed handkerchief
    And a painted china set—
Did your dolly hang her stocking up?
    What did your dolly get?

A VISIT FROM ST. NICHOLAS
by Clement Clarke Moore

'Twas the night before Christmas,
    when all through the house
Not a creature was stirring, not even a mouse;
The stockings were hung by the chimney
    with care,
In hopes that St. Nicholas soon
    would be there;
The children were nestled all snug in their beds,
While visions of sugar-plums danced
    in their heads;
And mamma in her 'kerchief, and I in my cap,
Had just settled our brains
    for a long winter's nap,
When out on the lawn there arose such a clatter,
I sprang from my bed to see what was the matter.
Away to the window I flew like a flash,
Tore open the shutters and threw up the sash.
The moon on the breast of the new-fallen snow
Gave the lustre of mid-day to objects below,
When, what to my wondering eyes should appear,
But a miniature sleigh, and eight tiny reindeer,
With a little old driver, so lively and quick,
I knew in a moment it must be St. Nick.
More rapid than eagles his coursers they came,
And he whistled, and shouted,
    and called them by name:

"Now, Dasher! now, Dancer!
      now, Prancer and Vixen!
On, Comet! on, Cupid!
      on, Donner and Blitzen!
To the top of the porch!
      to the top of the wall!
Now dash away! dash away! dash away all!"
As dry leaves that before the wild
      hurricane fly,
When they meet with an obstacle, mount to the
sky,
So up to the house-top the coursers they flew,
With a sleigh full of toys, and St. Nicholas too.
And then, in a twinkling, I heard on the roof
The prancing and pawing of each little hoof.
As I drew in my head, and was
      turning around,
Down the chimney St. Nicholas
      came with a bound.
He was dressed all in fur, from his head
      to his foot,
And his clothes were all tarnished
      with ashes and soot;
A bundle of toys he had flung on his back,
And he looked like a peddlar just
      opening his pack.
His eyes—how they twinkled! his dimples
      how merry!
His cheeks were like roses, his nose
      like a cherry!

His droll little mouth was drawn up like a bow,
And the beard of his chin was as white
    as the snow!
The stump of a pipe he held tight in his teeth,
And the smoke it encircled his head
    like a wreath;
He had a broad face and a little round belly,
That shook when he laughed, like a
    bowlful of jelly.
He was chubby and plump, a right jolly old elf,
And I laughed when I saw him,
    in spite of myself;
A wink of his eye and a twist of his head,
Soon gave me to know I had nothing to dread;
He spoke not a word, but went straight
    to work,
And filled all the stockings; then turned
    with a jerk,
And laying his finger aside of his nose,
And giving a nod, up the chimney he rose;
He sprang to his sleigh, to his team
    gave a whistle,
And away they all flew like the down
    of a thistle.
But I heard him exclaim, ere he drove
    out of sight,
"Happy Christmas to all, and to all
    a good-night."

Flowers and Forests

THE WORLD
by William Brighty Rands

Great, wide, beautiful, wonderful world,
With the wonderful water around you curled,
And the wonderful grass upon your breast—
World, you are beautifully dressed.

The wonderful air is over me,
And the wonderful wind is shaking the tree,
It walks on the water and whirls the mills,
And talks to itself on the tops of the hills.

You friendly Earth! How far you go,
With the wheat-fields that nod and the rivers that
     flow,
With cities and gardens, and cliffs and isles,
And people upon you for thousands of miles!

Ah! you are so great, and I am so small,
I tremble to think of you, World, at all;
And yet when I said my prayers to-day,
A whisper inside me seemed to say,
"You are more than the Earth, though you are
     such a dot:
You can love and think, and the Earth cannot!"

FOOLISH FLOWERS
by Rupert Sargent Holland

We've foxgloves in our garden;
　　How careless they must be
To leave their gloves out hanging
　　Where everyone can see!

And Bachelors leave their Buttons
　　In the same careless way,
If I should do the same with mine,
　　What would mother say?

We've lots of Larkspurs in the Yard—
　　Larks only fly and sing—
Birds surely don't need spurs because
　　They don't ride anything!

And as for Johnny-Jump-Ups—
　　I saw a hornet light
On one of them the other day,
　　He didn't jump a mite!

CATKIN

I have a little pussy,
    And her coat is silver grey;
She lives in a great wide meadow
    And she never runs away.
She always is a pussy,
    She'll never be a cat
Because—she's a pussy willow!
    Now what do you think of that?

COBWEBS

Dainty fairy lace-work, O so finely spun,
Lying on the grasses and shining in the sun,
Guess the fairies washed you and spread you out
    to dry,
And left you there a-glistening and a'shining to
    the sky!

TREES

by *Joyce Kilmer*

I think that I shall never see
A poem lovely as a tree.

A tree whose hungry mouth is pressed
Against the earth's sweet flowing breast;

A tree that looks at God all day
And lifts her leafy arms to pray;

A tree that may in summer wear
A nest of robins in her hair;

Upon whose bosom snow has lain;
Who intimately lives with rain.

Poems are made by fools like me,
But only God can make a tree.

OUT IN THE FIELDS

The little cares that fretted me,
    I lost them yesterday
Among the fields above the sea,
    Among the winds that play,
Among the lowing of the herds,
    The rustling of the trees,
Among the singing of the birds,
    The humming of the bees.

The foolish fears of what might pass
    I cast them all away
Among the clover-scented grass,
    Among the new-mown hay,
Among the hushing of the corn,
    Where drowsy poppies nod,
Where ill thoughts die and good are born—
    Out in the fields of God.

OH! LOOK AT THE MOON
by *Eliza Lee Follen*

Oh! look at the moon,
    She is shining up there;
Oh! mother, she looks
    Like a lamp in the air.

Last week she was smaller,
    And shaped like a bow;
But now she's grown bigger,
    And round as an O.

Pretty moon, pretty moon,
    How you shine on the door,
And make it all bright
    On my nursery floor!

You shine on my playthings,
    And show me their place,
And I love to look up
    At your pretty bright face.

And there is a star
    Close by you, and may be
That small, twinkling star
    Is your little baby.

STARS

A little boy sat dreaming
    Upon his mother's lap,
That all the stars up in the sky
    Fell down into his hat.

But when the dream was over,
    What did the dreamer do?
Why, he looked into his hat,
    And found it wasn't true.

THE GRASS
by Emily Dickinson

The grass so little has to do—
    A sphere of simple green,
With only butterflies to brood,
    And bees to entertain,

And stir all day to pretty tunes
    The breezes fetch along,
And hold the sunshine in its lap
    And bow to everything;

And thread the dews all night, like pearls,
    And make itself so fine,—
A duchess were too common
    For such a noticing.

And even when it dies, to pass
    In odours so divine,
As lowly spices gone to sleep,
    Or amulets of pine.

And then to dwell in sovereign barns,
    And dream the days away,—
The grass so little has to do,
    I wish I were the hay!

JACK-IN-THE-PULPIT
by Rupert Sargent Holland

Four of us went to the woods one day,
Keeping the trail in the Indian way,
   Creeping, crawling,
   Sometimes sprawling,
Pushing through bushes; and there we found
A little green pulpit stuck in the ground
And in the pulpit a brown man stood,
Preaching to all the folk in the wood.

We lay as quiet as Indians do,
Because each one of the four of us knew,
   At any sound,
   The creatures 'round,
The squirrels and chipmunks, birds and bees,
Would fly away through the ring of trees,
And Jack-in-the-Pulpit would stop his speech
If he knew we four were in easy reach.

We listened as hard as ever we could,
But not a one of us understood,
   Or even heard,
   A single word,
Though I saw a chipmunk nod his head
As if he knew what the preacher said,
And a big gray squirrel clapped his paws
When he thought it was time for some applause.

Many and many a Jack we've found,
But none of us ever heard a sound;
    So I suppose
    That Jackie knows
When children try to hear him preach,
And talks in some peculiar speech;
I wonder if we could find a way
To hear what Jacks-in-the-Pulpit say?

PIPPA'S SONG
by Robert Browning

The year's at the spring
And day's at the morn;
Morning's at seven;
The hillside's dew-pearled;
The lark's on the wing;
The snail's on the thorn;
God's in his heaven—
All's right with the world.

FREDDIE AND THE CHERRY TREE
by Ann Hawkshawe

Freddie saw some fine ripe cherries
    Hanging on a cherry tree.
And he said, "You pretty cherries,
    Will you not come down to me?"

"Thank you kindly," said a cherry,
    "We would rather stay up here;
If we ventured down this morning,
    You would eat us up, I fear."

One, the finest of the cherries,
    Dangled from a slender twig.
"You are beautiful," said Freddie,
    "Red and ripe, and oh, how big!"

"Catch me," said the cherry, "catch me,
    Little master, if you can."
"I would catch you soon," said Freddie,
    "If I were a grown-up man."

Freddie jumped, and tried to reach it,
    Standing high upon his toes;
But the cherry bobbed about,
    And laughed, and tickled Freddie's nose.

"Never mind," said little Freddie,
    "I shall have them when it's right."
But a blackbird whistled boldly,
    "I shall eat them all to-night."

THE OAK
by Mary Elliott

Observe, dear George, this nut is small;
  The Acorn is its name;
Would you suppose yon tree so tall
  From such a trifle came?

The Acorn, buried in the earth,
  When many years are past
Becomes the oak of matchless worth,
  Whose strength will ages last.

In Summer, pleasant is its shade,
  But greater far its use;
The wood which forms our ships for trade
  Its body can produce.

And many other things beside,
  I cannot now explain;
For where its merits have been tried,
  They were not tried in vain.

MR. FINNEY'S TURNIP

Mr. Finney had a turnip
    And it grew behind the barn;
And it grew and it grew,
    And that turnip did no harm.

There it grew and it grew
    Till it could grow no longer;
Then his daughter Lizzie picked it up
    And put it in the cellar.

There it lay and it lay
    Till it began to rot;
And his daughter Susie took it
    And put it in the pot.

And they boiled it and boiled it
    As long as they were able;
And then his daughters took it
    And put it on the table.

Mr. Finney and his wife
    They sat them down to sup;
And they ate and they ate
    And they ate that turnip up.

DANDELION

There was a pretty dandelion
    With lovely, fluffy hair,
That glistened in the sunshine
    And in the summer air.
But oh! this pretty dandelion
    Soon grew old and grey;
And, sad to tell! her charming hair
    Blew many miles away.

TO MAKE A PRAIRIE
by Emily Dickinson

To make a prairie it takes a clover
    and one bee,—
One clover, and a bee,
And revery.
The revery alone will do
If bees are few.

Fish, Fowl, and Fur

THE CITY MOUSE AND THE COUNTRY MOUSE
by Christina Georgina Rosetti

The city mouse lives in a house;—
    The garden mouse lives in a bower,
He's friendly with the frogs and toads,
    And sees the pretty plants in flower.

The city mouse eats bread and cheese;—
    The garden mouse eats what he can;
We will not grudge him seeds and stocks;
    Poor little timid furry man.

THE COW
by Ann and Jane Taylor

Thank you, pretty cow, that made
Pleasant milk to soak my bread,
Every day, and every night,
Warm, and fresh, and sweet, and white.

Do not chew the hemlock rank,
Growing on the weedy bank;
But the yellow cowslips eat,
They will make it very sweet.

Where the purple violet grows,
Where the bubbling water flows,
Where the grass is fresh and fine,
Pretty cow, go there and dine.

CONTENTMENT
by Eugene Field

Once on a time an old red hen
    Went strutting round with pompous clucks,
For she had little babies ten,
    A part of which were tiny ducks.
" 'Tis very rare that hens," said she,
    "Have baby ducks as well as chicks—
But I possess, as you can see,
    Of chickens four and ducklings six!"

A season later, this old hen
    Appeared, still cackling of her luck,
For, though she boasted babies ten,
    Not one among them was a duck!
" 'Tis well," she murmured, brooding o'er
    The little chicks of fleecy down,
"My babies now will stay ashore,
    And, consequently, cannot drown!"

The following spring the old red hen
    Clucked just as proudly as of yore—
But lo! her babies were ducklings ten,
    Instead of chickens as before!
" 'Tis better," said the old red hen,
    As she surveyed her waddling brood;
"A little water now and then
    Will surely do my darlings good!"

But oh! alas, how very sad!
　　When gentle spring rolled round again,
The eggs eventuated bad,
　　And childless was the old red hen!
Yet patiently she bore her woe,
　　And still she wore a cheerful air,
And said: " 'Tis best these things are so,
　　For babies are a dreadful care!"

I half suspect that many men,
　　And many, many women too,
Could learn a lesson from the hen
　　With plumage of vermilion hue.
She ne'er presumed to take offence
　　At any fate that might befall,
But meekly bowed to Providence—
　　She was contented—that was all!

THE KITTEN AT PLAY
by William Wordsworth

See the kitten on the wall,
Sporting with the leaves that fall,
Withered leaves, one, two, and three
Falling from the elder-tree,
Through the calm and frosty air
Of the morning bright and fair.

See the kitten, how she starts,
Crouches, stretches, paws and darts;
With a tiger-leap half way
Now she meets her coming prey.
Lets it go as fast and then
Has it in her power again.

Now she works with three or four,
Like an Indian conjurer;
Quick as he in feats of art,
Gracefully she plays her part;
Yet were gazing thousands there,
What would little Tabby care?

THE LION AND THE MOUSE
by *Jeffreys Taylor*

A lion with the heat oppress'd,
One day composed himself to rest;
But whilst he dozed, as he intended,
A mouse his royal back ascended;
Nor thought of harm, as Aesop tells,
Mistaking him for someone else;
And travell'd over him, and round him,
And might have left him as she found him
Had she not—tremble when you hear—
Tried to explore the monarch's ear!
Who straightaway woke, with wrath immense,
And shook his head to cast her thence.
"You rascal, what are you about?"
Said he, when he had turned her out.
"I'll teach you soon," the lion said,
"To make a mouse-hole in my head!"
So saying, he prepared his foot
To crush the trembling tiny brute;
But she (the mouse) with tearful eye,
Implored the lion's clemency,
Who thought it best at last to give
His little pris'ner a reprieve.
'Twas nearly twelve months after this,
The lion chanced his way to miss;
When pressing forward, heedless yet,
He got entangled in a net.
With dreadful rage, he stampt and tore,
And straight commenced a lordly roar;

When the poor mouse, who heard the noise,
Attended, for she knew his voice.
Then what the lion's utmost strength
Could not effect, she did at length;
With patient labour she applied
Her teeth, the network to divide;
And so at last forth issued he,
A *lion*, by a mouse set free.

Few are so small or weak, I guess,
But may assist us in distress,
Nor shall we ever, if we're wise,
The meanest, or the least despise.

THE COW AND THE ASS
by Jane Taylor

Beside a green meadow a stream used to flow,
So clear, you might see the white pebbles
   below.
To this cooling brook the warm cattle
   would stray,
To stand in the shade, on a hot summer's day.

A cow, quite oppressed by the heat of the sun,
Came here to refresh, as she often had done;
And, standing quite still, stooping
   over the stream,
Was musing, perhaps; or perhaps
   she might dream.

But soon a brown ass of respectable look
Came trotting up also, to taste of the brook,
And to nibble a few of the daisies and grass;
"How d'ye do?" said the Cow.—
  "How d'ye do?" said the Ass.

"Take a seat!" said the Cow, gently waving
   her hand.
"By no means, dear Madam," said he, "while
   you stand!"
Then, stooping to drink with a complaisant bow,
"Ma'am, your health!" said the Ass.
  "Thank you, Sir!" said the Cow.

When a few of these compliments more
          had been passed,
They laid themselves down on the herbage
          at last;
And waiting politely—as gentlemen must—
The ass held his tongue, that the cow
          might speak first.

Then with a deep sigh, she directly began:
"Don't you think, Mr. Ass, we are injured
          by man?
'Tis a subject which lies with a weight
          on my mind:
We really are greatly oppressed by mankind.

"Pray what is the reason—I see none at all—
That I always must go when Suke chooses
          to call?
Whatever I'm doing—'tis certainly hard!—
I'm forced to leave off to be milked
          in the yard.

"I've no will of my own, but must do
          as they please,
And give them my milk to make butter and
          cheese:
I've often a great mind to kick down the pail,
Or give Suke a box on the ear with my tail!"

"But, Ma'am," said the Ass, "not presuming
        to teach—
Oh dear! I beg pardon—pray finish your speech:
I thought you had finished, in deed,"
        said the Swain;
"Go on, and I'll not interrupt you again."

"Why, Sir, I was just then about to observe,
I'm resolved that these tyrants no longer
        I'll serve;
But leave them forever to do as they please,
And look somewhere else for their butter
        and cheese."

Ass waited a moment to see if she'd done,
And then, "Not presuming to teach," he begun,
"With submission, dear Madam, to your
        better wit,
I own I am not quite convinced by it yet.

"That you're of great service to them
        is quite true,
But surely they are of some service to you;
'Tis their pleasant meadow in which you regale,
They feed you in winter when grass
        and weeds fail.

"And then a warm covert they always provide,
Dear Madam, to shelter your delicate hide.
For my own part, I know I receive
     much from man,
And for him, in return, I do all I can."

The Cow, upon this, cast her eyes on the grass,
Not pleased at thus being reproved by an Ass;
"Yet," thought she, "I'm determined
     I'll benefit by 't;
I really believe that the fellow is right!"

THE SHEEP
by Ann Taylor

Lazy sheep, pray tell me why
In the grassy fields you lie,
Eating grass and daisies white,
From the morning till the night?
Every thing can something do,
But what kind of use are you?

Nay, my little master, nay,
Do not serve me so, I pray;
Don't you see the wool that grows
On my back to make you clothes?
Cold, and very cold you'd get,
If I did not give you it.

Sure it seems a pleasant thing
To nip the daisies in the spring,
But many chilly nights I pass
On the cold and dewy grass,
Or pick a scanty dinner where
All the common's brown and bare.

Then the farmer comes at last,
When the merry spring is past,
And cuts my woolly coat away
To warm you in the winter's day;
Little master, this is why
In the grassy fields I lie.

THE CANARY
by Elizabeth Turner

Mary had a little bird,
    With feathers bright and yellow,
Slender legs—upon my word,
    He was a pretty fellow!

Sweetest notes he always sung,
    Which much delighted Mary;
Often when his cage was hung,
    She sat to hear Canary.

Crumb of bread and dainty seeds
    She carried to him daily:
Seeking for the early weeds,
    She deck'd his palace gaily.

This, my little readers, learn,
    And ever practice duly;
Songs and smiles of love return
    To friends who love you truly.

TWENTY FROGGIES
by George Cooper

Twenty froggies went to school
Down beside a rushy pool.
Twenty little coats of green,
Twenty vests all white and clean.

"We must be in time," said they,
First we study, then we play";
"That is how we keep the rule,
When we froggies go to school."

Master Bull-frog, brave and stern,
Called his classes in their turn,
Taught them how to nobly strive,
Also how to leap and dive;

Taught them how to dodge a blow,
From the sticks that bad boys throw.
Twenty froggies grew up fast,
Bull-frogs they became at last;

Polished to a high degree,
As each froggie ought to be,
Now they sit on other logs,
Teaching other little frogs.

MISTER FLY
by *Thomas Miller*

What a sharp little fellow is Mister Fly,
He goes where he pleases, low or high,
And can walk just as well with his feet to the sky
    As I can on the floor;
    At the window he comes
    With a buzz and a roar,
    And o'er the smooth glass
    Can easily pass
    Or through the keyhole of the door.
He eats the sugar, and goes away,
Nor ever once asks what there is to pay;
And sometimes he crosses the teapot's steam,
And comes and plunges his head in the cream;
Then on the edge of the jug he stands,
And cleans his wings with his feet and hands.
This done, through the window he hurries away,
And gives a buzz, as if to say,
"At present I haven't a minute to stay,
But I'll peep in again in the course of the day."
    Then again he'll fly
    Where the sunbeams lie,
    And neither stop to shake hands
    Nor bid goodbye:
Such a strange little fellow is Master Fly,
Who goes where he pleases, low or high,
    And can walk on the ceiling
    Without ever feeling
A fear of tumbling down "sky-high."

THE BROWN THRUSH
by *Lucy Larcom*

There's a merry brown thrush sitting up
    in the tree.
He's singing to me! He's singing to me!
And what does he say, little girl, little boy?
"Oh, the world's running over with joy!
    Don't you hear? Don't you see?
    Hush! Look! In my tree,
    I'm as happy as happy can be!"

And the brown thrush keeps singing,
    "A nest do you see
And five eggs, hid by me in the juniper tree?
Don't meddle! Don't touch! little girl,
    little boy,
Or the world will lose some of its joy!
    Now I'm glad! Now I'm free!
    And always shall be,
    If you never bring sorrow to me."

So the merry brown thrush sings away
    in the tree,
To you and to me, to you and to me;
And he sings all the day, little girl,
    little boy,
"Oh, the world's running over with joy!
    But long it won't be
    Don't you know? Don't you see?
    Unless we're as good as can be."

THE SNAIL
by William Cowper

To grass or leaf, or fruit or wall,
The snail sticks close, nor fears to fall,
As if he grew there, house and all
      Together.

Within that house secure he hides,
When danger imminent betides,
Of storm, or other harm besides
      Of weather.

Give but his horns the slightest touch,
His self-collecting power is such,
He shrinks into his house with much
      Displeasure.

Where'er he dwells, he dwells alone,
Except himself, has chattels none,
Well satisfied to be his own
      Whole treasure.

Thus, hermit-like, his life he leads,
Nor partner of his banquet needs,
And if he meets one, only feeds
      The faster.

Who seeks him must be worse than blind
(He and his house are so combined),
If, finding it, he fails to find
      Its master.

THE LOBSTER AND THE MAID
by Frederick Edward Weatherly

He was a gentle lobster
    (The boats had just come in),
He did not love the fishermen,
    He could not stand their din;
And so he quietly stole off,
    As if it were no sin.

She was a little maiden,
    He met her on the sand,
"And how d'you do?" the lobster said
    "Why don't you give your hand?"
For why she edged away from him
    He *could* not understand.

"Excuse me, sir," the maiden said:
    "Excuse me, if you please,"
And put her hands behind her back,
    And doubled up her knees;
"I always thought that lobsters were
    A little apt to squeeze."

"Your ignorance," the lobster said,
    "Is natural, I fear;
Such scandal is a shame," he sobbed,
    "It is not true, my dear,"
And with his pocket-handkerchief
    He wiped away a tear.

So out she put her little hand,
    As though she feared him not,
When some one grabbed him suddenly
    And put him in a pot,
With water which, I think he found
    Uncomfortably hot.

It may have been the water made
    The blood flow to his head,
It may have been that dreadful fib
    Lay on his soul like lead;
This much is true—he went in grey,
    And came out very red.

KING BRUCE AND THE SPIDER
by Eliza Cook

King Bruce of Scotland flung himself down
    In a lonely mood to think;
'Tis true he was a monarch, and wore a crown,
    But his heart was beginning to sink.

For he had been trying to do a great deed,
    To make his people glad;
He had tried, and tried, but couldn't succeed;
    And so he became quite sad.

He flung himself down in low despair,
    As grieved as a man could be;
And after a while as he pondered there,
    "I'll give it all up," said he.

Now just at that moment a spider dropp'd
    With its silken cobweb clue;
And the king in the midst of his thinking
      stopp'd
    To see what the spider would do.

'Twas a long way up to the ceiling dome,
    And it hung by a rope so fine;
That how it could get to its cobweb home
    King Bruce could not divine.

It soon began to cling and crawl
    Straight up with strong endeavor;
But down it came with a slippery sprawl,
    As near the ground as ever.

Up, up it ran, not a second it stay'd
    To utter the least complaint;
Till it fell still lower, and there it laid,
    A little dizzy and faint.

Its head grew steady—again it went,
    And travell'd a half-yard higher;
'Twas a delicate thread it had to tread,
    A road where its feet would tire.

Again it fell and swung below,
    But again it quickly mounted;
Till up and down, now fast, now slow,
    Nine brave attempts were counted.

"Sure," cried the King, "that foolish thing
    Will strive no more to climb;
When it toils so hard to reach and cling,
    And tumbles every time."

But up the insect went once more,
    Ah me! 'tis an anxious minute;
He's only a foot from his cobweb door,
    Oh, say will he lose or win it!

Steadily, steadily, inch by inch
    Higher and higher he got;
And a bold little run at the very last pinch
    Put him into his native cot.

"Bravo, bravo!" the King cried out,
    "All honour to those who try;
The spider up there defied despair;
    He conquer'd, and why shouldn't I?"

And Bruce of Scotland braced his mind,
    And gossips tell the tale,
That he tried once more as he tried before,
    And that time did not fail.

Pay goodly heed, all ye who read,
    And beware of saying, "I can't;"
'Tis a cowardly word, and apt to lead
    To Idleness, Folly, and Want.

Whenever you find your heart despair
    Of doing some goodly thing;
Con over this strain, try bravely again,
    And remember the Spider and King.

THE ANT AND THE CRICKET

A silly young cricket, accustomed to sing
Through the warm, sunny months of gay summer
     and spring,
Began to complain, when he found that at home
His cupboard was empty and winter was come.
    Not a crumb to be found
    On the snow-covered ground;
    Not a flower could he see
    Not a leaf on a tree:
"Oh, what will become," says the cricket, "of me?"

At last by starvation and famine made bold,
All dripping with wet and all trembling
      with cold,
Away he set off to a miserly ant,
To see if, to keep him alive, he would grant
    Him shelter from rain:
    A mouthful of grain
    He wished only to borrow,
    He'd repay it to-morrow:
If not, he must die of starvation and sorrow.

Says the ant to the cricket, "I'm your servant
     and friend,
But we ants never borrow, we ants never lend;
But tell me, dear sir, did you lay nothing by
When the weather was warm?" Said the cricket,
     "Not I.
    My heart was so light
    That I sang day and night,
    For all nature looked gay."

"You sang, sir, you say?
Go then," said the ant, "and dance winter away."
Thus ending, he hastily lifted the wicket,
And out of the door turned the poor
              little cricket.
Though this is a fable, the moral is good:
If you live without work, you must live
              without food.

THE BUTTERFLY'S BALL
by William Roscoe

Come, take up your hats, and away let us haste
To the Butterfly's ball and the
      Grasshopper's feast;
The trumpeter Gadfly has summon'd the crew,
And the revels are now only waiting for you.

On the smooth shaven grass by the side
      of the wood,
Beneath a broad oak that for ages has stood,
See the children of earth, and the tenants
      of air,
For an evening's amusement together repair.

And there came the Beetle, so blind
      and so black,
Who carried the Emmet, his friend,
      on his back;
And there was the Gnat,
      and the Dragon-fly too,
With all their relations, green, orange,
      and blue.

And there came the Moth in his plummage
      of down,
And the Hornet in jacket of yellow
      and brown,
Who with him the Wasp his companion
      did bring,
But they promised that evening to lay
      by their sting.

And the sly little Dormouse crept out
      of his hole,
And led to the feast his blind brother
      the Mole;
And the Snail, with his horns peeping out
      from his shell,
Came from a great distance—the length
      of an ell.

A mushroom their table, and on it was laid
A water dock leaf, with a table-cloth made;
The viands were various, to each
      of their taste,
And the Bee brought his honey to crown
      the repast.

There close on his haunches, so solemn
      and wise,
The Frog from a corner look'd up
      to the skies;
And the Squirrel well-pleased such diversion
      to see,
Sat cracking his nuts overhead in a tree.

Then out came the Spider, with fingers
      so fine,
To show his dexterity on the tight line;
From one branch to another his cobwebs
      he slung,
Then as quick as an arrow he darted along.

But just in the middle, oh! shocking to tell!
From his rope in an instant poor Harlequin
      fell;
Yet he touch'd not the ground, but
      with talons outspread,
Hung suspended in air at the end
      of a thread.

Then the Grasshopper came with a jerk
      and a spring,
Very long was his leg, though but short
      was his wing;
He took but three leaps, and was soon
      out of sight,
And chirp'd his own praises the rest
      of the night.

With step so majestic the Snail did advance,
And promised the gazers a minuet to dance;
But they all laugh'd so loud that he pull'd
      in his head,
And went to his own little chamber to bed.

Then as evening gave way to the shadows
      of night,
The watchman, the Glow-worm, came out
      with his light;
Then home let us hasten while yet we can see,
For no watchman is waiting for you and for me.

THE SPIDER AND THE FLY
by Mary Howitt

"Will you walk into my parlour?"
      said the Spider to the Fly,
" 'Tis the prettiest little parlour
      that ever you did spy;
The way into my parlour is up a winding stair,
And I have many curious things to show
      when you are there."
"Oh, no, no,! said the little Fly; "to ask me is
      in vain;
For who goes up your winding stair can ne'er
      come down again."
"I'm sure you must be weary, dear,
      with soaring up so high;
Will you rest upon my little bed?"
      said the Spider to the Fly.
"There are pretty curtains drawn around;
      the sheets are fine and thin,
And if you like to rest awhile, I'll
      snugly tuck you in!"
"Oh, no, no," said the little Fly,
      "for I've often heard it said,
They never, never wake again,
      who sleep upon your bed!"
Said the cunning Spider to the Fly:
      "Dear friend, what can I do,
To prove the warm affection I've always
      felt for you!
I have within my pantry good store of all
      that's nice;

I'm sure you're very welcome—will you please
      to take a slice?"
"Oh, no, no," said the little Fly, "kind sir,
      that cannot be,
I've heard what's in your pantry, and I
      do not wish to see!"
"Sweet creature!" said the Spider,
      "you're witty and you're wise,
How handsome are your gauzy wings,
      how brilliant are your eyes;
I have a little looking-glass upon
      my parlour shelf,
If you'll step in one moment, dear,
      you shall behold yourself."
"I thank you, gentle sir," she said,
      "for what you're pleased to say,
And bidding you good morning
      now, I'll call another day."

The Spider turned him roundabout,
      and went into his den,
For well he knew the silly Fly would soon
      come back again:
So he wove a subtle web in a little
      corner sly,
And set his table ready to dine
      upon the Fly.
Come hither, hither, pretty Fly,
      with the pearl and silver wing;
Your robes are green and purple—there's
      a crest upon your head;
Your eyes are like the diamond bright,
      but mine are dull as lead!"

Alas, alas! how very soon this silly
    little Fly,
Hearing his wily, flattering words,
    came slowly flitting by;
With buzzing wings she hung aloft,
    then near and nearer drew,
Thinking only of her brilliant eyes,
    and green and purple hue—
Thinking only of her crested head—
    poor foolish thing!—at last
Up jump'd the cunning Spider, and fiercely
    held her fast.
He dragg'd her up his winding stair,
    into his dismal den,
Within his little parlour—but she ne'er
    came out again!

And now, dear little children, who may
    this story read,
To idle, silly, flattering words, I pray
    you ne'er give heed:
Unto an evil counsellor close heart and ear
    and eye,
And take this lesson from this tale,
    of the Spider and the Fly.

HOW DOTH THE LITTLE BUSY BEE
by Isaac Watts

How doth the little busy bee
    Improve each shining hour,
And gather honey all the day
    From every opening flow'r!

How skillfully she builds her cell!
    How neat she spreads the wax!
And labours hard to store it well
    With the sweet food she makes.

In works of labour or of skill,
    I would be busy too;
For Satan finds some mischief still
    For idle hands to do.

In books, or work, or healthful play,
    Let my first years be past,
That I may give for ev'ry day
    Some good account at last.

SUCH WISDOM

Though tiny things, ants must see very well;
They must have been carefully taught how to
      smell;
Because when my mother makes cookies or pie
They find out about it much sooner than I!

AN OLD RAT'S TALE

He was a rat, and she was a rat;
　　And down in one hole they did dwell;
And both were as black as a witch's cat,
　　And they loved each other well.

He had a tail and she had a tail,
　　Both long and curling and fine;
And each said, "Yours is the finest tail
　　In the world excepting mine."

He smelt the cheese, and she smelt the cheese,
　　And they both pronounced it good;
And both remarked it would greatly add
　　To the charms of their daily food.

So he ventured out, and she ventured out,
　　And I saw them go with pain;
But what befell them I never can tell,
　　For they never came back again.

Manners and Morals

THE GREEDY PIGGY THAT ATE TOO FAST
by Eliza Grove

Oh! Piggy, what was in your trough
That thus you raise your head and cough?
Was it a rough, a crooked bone,
That cookey in the pail had thrown?
Speak, Piggy, Speak! and tell me plain
What 'tis that seems to cause you pain."

"Oh, thank you sir! I will speak out
As soon as I can clear my throat.
This morning, when I left my sty,
So eager for my food was I,
That I began my rich repast—
I blush to own it—rather fast;
And, what with haste, sir, and ill-luck,
A something in my poor throat stuck,
Which I discover'd very soon
To be a silver table-spoon.
This, sir, is all—no other tale
Have I against the kitchen-pail."

"I hope it is; but I must own
I'm sorry for my table-spoon;
And scarcely can I overlook
The carelessness of Mistress Cook.
But, Piggy, profit by your pain,
And do not eat so fast again."

THERE WAS A LITTLE GIRL

There was a little girl, who had a little curl,
    Right in the middle of her forehead,
And when she was good, she was very, very good.
    But when she was bad she was horrid.

She stood on her head, on her little trundle-bed,
    With nobody by for to hinder;
She screamed and she squalled, she yelled and
        she bawled,
    And drummed her little heels against the
        winder.

Her mother heard the noise, and thought it was
        the boys
    Playing in the empty attic,
She rushed upstairs, and caught her unawares,
    And spanked her, most emphatic.

THE REFORMATION OF GODFREY GORE
by William Brighty Rands

Godfrey Gordon Gustavus Gore—
No doubt you have heard the name before—
Was a boy who never would shut a door!

The wind might whistle, the wind might roar,
And teeth be aching and throats be sore,
But still he never would shut the door.

His father would beg, his mother implore,
"Godfrey Gordon Gustavus Gore,
We really do wish you would shut the door!"

Their hands they wrung, their hair they tore;
But Godfrey Gordon Gustavus Gore
Was deaf as the buoy out at the Nore.

When he walked forth the folks would roar,
"Godfrey Gordon Gustavus Gore,
Whey don't you think to shut the door?"

They rigged out a Shutter with sail and oar,
And threatened to pack off Gustavus Gore
On a voyage of penance to Singapore.
But he begged for mercy, and said, "No more!
Pray do not send me to Singapore
On a Shutter, and then I will shut the door!"

"You will?" said his parents;
     "then keep on shore!
But mind you do! For the plague is sore
Of a fellow that never will shut the door,
Godfrey Gordon Gustavus Gore!"

THE CASTLE BUILDER
by *Jean de La Fontaine*

It happened on a summer's day,
A country lass as fresh as May,
Decked in a wholesome russet gown,
Was going to the market town;
So blithe her looks so simply clean,
You'd take her for a May-day queen;
Though for her garland, says the tale,
Her head sustained a loaded pail.
As on her way she passed along,
She hummed the fragments of a song;
She did not hum for want of thought—
Quite pleased with what to sale she brought,
She reckoned by her own account,
When all was sold, the whole amount.
Thus she—"In time this little ware
May turn to great account, with care:
My milk being sold for—so and so,
I'll buy some eggs as markets go,
And set them;—at the time I fix,
These eggs will bring as many chicks;
I'll spare no pains to feed them well;
They'll bring vast profit when they sell.
With this, I'll buy a little pig,
And when 'tis grown up fat and big,
I'll sell it, whether boar or sow,
And with the money buy a cow:
This cow will surely have a calf,
And there the profit's half in half;
Besides there's butter, milk, and cheese,
To keep the market when I please:

All which I'll sell, and buy a farm,
Then shall of sweethearts have a swarm.
Oh! then for ribands, gloves, and rings!
Ay! more than twenty pretty things—
One brings me this, another that,
And I shall have—I know no what!"
Fired with the thought—the sanguine lass!—
Of what was thus to come to pass,
Her heart beat strong; she gave a bound,
And down came milk-pail on the ground:
Eggs, fowls, pig, hog (ah, well-a-day!)
Cow, calf, and farm—all swam away!

THE STORY OF AUGUSTUS
WHO WOULD NOT HAVE ANY SOUP
by Heinrich Hoffmann

Augustus was a chubby lad;
Fat ruddy cheeks Augustus had;
And everybody saw with joy,
The plump and hearty healthy boy.
He ate and drank as he was told,
And never let his soup get cold.
But one day, one cold winter's day,
He scream'd out—"Take the soup away!
O take the nasty soup away!
I won't have any soup to-day!"

How lank and lean Augustus grows!
Next day he scarcely fills his clothes,
Yet, though he feels so weak and ill,
The naughty fellow cries out still—
"Not any soup for me, I say:
O take the nasty soup away!
I won't have any soup to-day!"

The third day comes; oh! what a sin!
To make himself so pale and thin.
Yet, when the soup is put on table,
He screams, as loud as he is able,
"Not any soup for me, I say:
O take the nasty soup away!
I won't have any soup to-day!"

Look at him, now the fourth day's come!
He scarcely weighs a sugar-plum;
He's like a little bit of thread,
And on the fifth day he was—dead!

THE GOOD GIRL
by Elizabeth Turner

Miss Lydia Banks, though very young,
Will never do what's rude or wrong;
When spoken to, she always tries
To give the most polite replies.

Observing what at school she's taught,
She turns her toes as children ought;
And when return'd at night from school
She never lolls on chair or stool.

Some children, when they write, we know,
Their ink about them heedless throw;
But she, though young, has learn'd to think,
That clothes look spoil'd with spots of ink.

Perhaps some little girl may ask,
If Lydia always learns her task;
With pleasure I can answer this,
Because with truth I answer, "Yes."

P'S AND Q'S

by Rupert Sargent Holland

It takes a lot of letters to make up the alphabet,
And two or three of them are very easy to forget;
There's K—a funny letter—and X and Y and Z—
There's hardly any use at all for any of those
      three!
The vowels are the busy ones, A, E, I, O, U—
They've twice the work that all the other letters
      have to do;
I don't know why it is that grown-up people al-
      ways choose
To tell us children to be sure and mind our P's
      and Q's.

They're funny looking letters, particularly Q,
It never goes around except in company with U;
P is much more important, it starts off pie and
      play,
It's not hard to remember if you think of it that
      way;
But lots of words begin with F and H and S and T,
They're just as worth remembering as any, seems
      to me;
Yet when we've strangers in the house, my par-
      ents always say,
"Be sure you don't forget to mind your P's and Q's
      to-day!"

MR. NOBODY

I know a funny little man,
    As quiet as a mouse,
Who does the mischief that is done
    In everybody's house!
There's no one ever sees his face,
    And yet we all agree
That every plate we break was cracked
    By Mr. Nobody.

'Tis he who always tears our books,
    Who leaves the door ajar,
He pulls the buttons from our shirts,
    And scatters pins afar;
That squeaking door will always squeak
    For, prithee, don't you see,
We leave the oiling to be done,
    By Mr. Nobody.

He puts damp wood upon the fire,
    That kettles cannot boil;
His are the feet that bring in mud,
    And all the carpets soil.
The papers always are mislaid,
    Who had them last but he?
There's no one tosses them about
    But Mr. Nobody.

The finger-marks upon the door
    By none of us are made;
We never leave the blinds unclosed,
    To let the curtains fade.
The ink we never spill, the boots
    That lying round you see
Are not our boots; they all belong
    To Mr. Nobody.

THE FOUNTAIN
by *James Russell Lowell*

Into the sunshine,
    Full of the light,
Leaping and flashing
    From morn till night!

Into the moonlight,
    Whiter than snow,
Waving so flower-like
    When the winds blow!

Into the starlight,
    Rushing in spray,
Happy at midnight,
    Happy by day!

Ever in motion,
    Blithesome and cheery,
Still climbing heavenward,
    Never aweary;

Glad of all weathers,
    Still seeming best,
Upward or downward
    Motion thy rest;

Full of a nature
    Nothing can tame,
Changed every moment,
    Ever the same;

Ceaseless aspiring,
    Ceaseless content,
Darkness or sunshine
    Thy element;

Glorious fountain!
    Let my heart be
Fresh, changeful, constant,
    Upward like thee!

NIGHT BLESSING

Good night,
Sleep tight,
Wake up bright
In the morning light
To do what's right
With all your might.

THREE THINGS TO REMEMBER
by William Blake

A Robin Redbreast in a cage,
Puts all Heaven in a rage.

A skylark wounded on the wing
Doth make a cherub cease to sing.

He who shall hurt the little wren
Shall never be beloved by men.

TIME TO RISE
by Robert Louis Stevenson

A birdie with a yellow bill
Hopped upon the window sill,
Cocked his shining eye, and said:
"Ain't you 'shamed, you sleepy-head?"

RULES OF BEHAVIOR

Hearts, like doors, will ope with ease
To very, very little keys,
And don't forget that two of these
Are "I thank you" and "If you please."

* * *

Come when you're called,
    Do what you're bid,
Close the door after you,
    Never be chid.

* * *

Seldom "can't"
    Seldom "don't;"
Never "shan't,"
    Never "won't."

* * *

Tommy's tears and Mary's fears
Will make them old before their years.

* * *

For every evil under the sun,
There is a remedy, or there is none;
If there be one, try to find it;
If there be none, never mind it.

He that would thrive must rise at
     five;
He that hath thriven may lie till
     seven.

*   *   *

Cock crows in the morning to tell
     us to rise,
And he who lies late will never be
     wise;
For early to bed and early to rise
Is the way to be healthy and
     wealthy and wise.

*   *   *

Do not loiter and be late,
Making other people wait;
Do not rudely point or touch:
Do not eat and drink too much:
Finish what you have before
You ever ask or send for more:
Never crumble or destroy
Food that others might enjoy;
They who idly *crumbs* will waste
Often want a loaf to taste!
Never spill your milk or tea,
Never rude or noisy be;
Never choose the daintiest food,
Be content with what is good:
Seek in all things that you can
To be a little gentleman.

DIRTY JIM
by *Jane Taylor*

There was one little Jim,
'Tis reported of him,
 And must be to his lasting disgrace,
That he never was seen
With hands at all clean,
 Nor yet ever clean was his face.

His friends were much hurt
To see so much dirt,
 And often they made him quite clean;
But all was in vain,
He got dirty again,
 And not at all fit to be seen.

It gave him no pain
To hear them complain,
 Nor his own dirty clothes to survey;
His indolent mind
No pleasure could find
 In tidy and wholesome array.

The idle and bad,
Like this little lad,
 May love dirty ways, to be sure;
But good boys are seen,
To be decent and clean,
 Although they are ever so poor.

JOHN WESLEY'S RULE

Do all the good you can,
In all the ways you can,
In all the places you can,
At all the times you can,
To all the people you can,
As long as ever you can.

LITTLE THINGS
by Julia Fletcher Carney

Little drops of water,
    Little grains of sand,
Make the mighty ocean
    And the pleasant land.

So the little moments,
    Humble though they be,
Make the mighty ages
    Of eternity.

So our little errors
    Lead the soul away
From the path of virtue,
    Far in sin to stray.

Little deeds of kindness,
    Little words of love,
Help to make earth happy
    Like the heaven above.

BIG AND LITTLE THINGS
by *Alfred H. Miles*

I cannot do the big things
    That I should like to do,
To make the earth for ever fair,
    The sky for ever blue.
But I can do the small things
    That help to make it sweet;
Tho' clouds arise and fill the skies,
    And tempests beat.

I cannot stay the rain-drops
    That tumble from the skies;
But I can wipe the tears away
    From baby's pretty eyes.

I cannot make the sun shine,
    Or warm the winter bleak;
But I can make the summer come
    On sister's rosy cheek.

I cannot stay the storm clouds,
    Or drive them from their place;
But I can clear the clouds away
    From brother's troubled face.

I cannot make the corn grow,
    Or work upon the land;
But I can put new strength and will
    In father's busy hand.

I cannot stay the east wind,
    Or thaw its icy smart;
But I can keep a corner warm
    In mother's loving heart.

I cannot do the big things
    That I should like to do,
To make the earth for ever fair,
    The sky for ever blue.
But I can do the small things
    That help to make it sweet;
Tho' clouds arise and fill the skies
    And tempests beat.

REBECCA'S AFTER-THOUGHT
by Elizabeth Turner

Yesterday, Rebecca Mason,
    In the parlor by herself,
Broke a handsome china basin,
    Placed upon the mantel-shelf.

Quite alarmed, she thought of going
    Very quietly away,
Not a single person knowing
    Of her being there that day.

But Rebecca recollected
    She was taught deceit to shun;
And the moment she reflected,
    Told her mother what was done;

Who commended her behavior,
Loved her better, and forgave her.

EXTREMES
by James Whitcomb Riley

A little boy once played so loud
That the Thunder, up in a thunder-cloud,
Said, "Since *I* can't be heard, why, then,
I'll never, never thunder again!"

And a little girl once kept so still
That she heard a fly on the window-sill
Whisper and say to a lady-bird,
"She's the stilliest child I ever heard!"

THE BLIND MEN AND THE ELEPHANT
by John Godfrey Saxe

It was six men of Indostan
    To learning much inclined,
Who went to see the Elephant
    (Though all of them were blind),
That each by observation
    Might satisfy his mind.

The *First* approached the Elephant,
    And happening to fall
Against his broad and sturdy side,
    At once began to bawl:
"God bless me! but the Elephant
    Is very like a wall!"

The *Second*, feeling of the tusk,
    Cried, "Ho! what have we here
So very round and smooth and sharp?
    To me 'tis mighty clear
This wonder of an Elephant
    Is very like a spear!"

The *Third* approached the animal,
    And happening to take
The squirming trunk within his hands,
    Thus boldly up and spake:
"I see," quoth he, "the Elephant
    Is very like a snake!"

The *Fourth* reached out an eager hand,
    And felt about the knee
"What most this wondrous beast is like
    Is mighty plain," quoth he;
"'Tis clear enough the Elephant
    Is very like a tree!"

The *Fifth* who chanced to touch the ear,
    Said: "E'en the blindest man
Can tell what this resemble most;
    Deny the fact who can,
This marvel of an Elephant
    Is very like a fan!"

The *Sixth* no sooner had begun
    About the beast to grope,
Then, seizing on the swinging tail
    That fell within his scope,
"I see," quoth he, "the Elephant
    Is very like a rope!"

And so these men of Indostan
    Disputed loud and long,
Each in his own opinion
    Exceeding stiff and strong,
Though each was partly in the right,
    And all were in the wrong!

Moral

So oft in theologic wars,
    The disputants, I ween,
Rail on in utter ignorance
Of what each other mean,
And prate about an Elephant
    Not one of them has seen!

WHAT IS GOOD?

by John Boyle O'Reilly

"What is the real good"
I asked in musing mood.

Order, said the law court;
Knowledge, said the school;
Truth, said the wise man;
Pleasure, said the fool;
Love, said the maiden;
Beauty, said the page;
Freedom, said the dreamer;
Home, said the sage;
Fame, said the soldier;
Equity, the seer;—

Spake my heart full sadly,
"The answer is not here."

Then within my bosom
Softly this I heard:
"Each heart holds the secret;
Kindness is the word."

Childhood Thoughts
and Merriment

TO A USURPER
by *Eugene Fields*

Aha! a traitor in the camp,
    A rebel strangely bold,—
A lisping, laughing, toddling scamp,
    Not more than four years old!

To think that I, who've ruled alone
    So proudly in the past,
Should be ejected from my throne
    By my own son at last!

He trots his treason to and fro,
    As only babies can,
And says he'll be his mamma's beau
    When he's a "gweat, big man"!

You stingy boy! you've always had
    A share in mamma's heart.
Would you begrudge your poor old dad
    The tiniest little part?

That mamma, I regret to see,
    Inclines to take your part.—
As if a dual monarchy
    Should rule her gentle heart!

But when the years of youth have sped,
    The bearded man, I trow,
Will quite forget he ever said
    He'd be his mamma's beau.

Renounce your treason, little son,
    Leave mamma's heart to me;
For there will come another one
    To claim your loyalty.

And when that other comes to you,
    God grant her love may shine
Through all your life, as fair and true
    As mamma's does through mine!

OUR MOTHER

Hundreds of stars in the pretty sky,
  Hundreds of shells on the shore together,
Hundreds of birds that go singing by,
  Hundreds of birds in the sunny weather,

Hundreds of dewdrops that greet the dawn,
  Hundreds of bees in the purple clover,
Hundreds of butterflies on the lawn,
  But only one mother the wide world over.

A BOY'S MOTHER
by *James Whitcomb Riley*

My mother she's so good to me,
Ef I was good as I could be,
I couldn't be as good—no, sir!—
Can't any boy be good as her!

She loves me when I'm glad er sad;
She loves me when I'm good er bad;
An', what's a funniest thing, she says
She loves me when she punishes.

I don't like her to punish me,—
That don't hurt—but it hurts to see
her cryin'.—Nen *I* cry; an' nen
We both cry and be good again.

She loves me when she cuts an' sews
My little cloak an' Sund'y clothes;
An' when my Pa comes home to tea,
She loves him most as much as me.

She laughs an' tells him all I said,
An' grabs me up an' pats my head;
An' I hug *her*, an' hug my Pa,
An' love him purt' nigh as much as Ma.

THE DUEL

by Eugene Fields

The gingham dog and the calico cat
Side by side on the table sat;
'Twas half-past twelve, and (what do you think!)
Nor one nor t'other had slept a wink!
    The old Dutch clock and the Chinese plate
    Appeared to know as sure as fate
There was going to be a terrible spat.
    (I wasn't there; I simply state
    What was told to me by the Chinese plate!)

The gingham dog went "bow-wow-wow!'
And the calico cat replied "mee-ow!"
The air was littered, an hour or so,
With bits of gingham and calico,
    While the old Dutch clock in the chimney-
        place
    Up with its hands before its face,
For it always dreaded a family row!
    (Now mind: I'm only telling you
    What the old Dutch clock declares is true!)

The Chinese plate looked very blue,
And wailed, "Oh, dear! what shall we do!"
But the gingham dog and the calico cat
Wallowed this way and tumbled that,
    Employing every tooth and claw
    In the awfullest way you ever saw—
And, oh! how the gingham and calico flew!
    (Don't fancy I exaggerate—
    I got my news from the Chinese plate!)

Next morning, where the two had sat
They found no trace of dog or cat;
And some folks think unto this day
That burglars stole that pair away!
 But the truth about the cat and pup
 Is this: they ate each other up!
Now what do you really think of that!
 (The old Dutch clock it told me so,
 And that is how I came to know.)

THE LAND OF NOD

by *Robert Louis Stevenson*

From breakfast on through all the day
At home among my friends I stay;
But every night I go abroad
Afar into the land of Nod.

All by myself I have to go,
With none to tell me what to do—
All alone beside the streams
And up the mountain-sides of dreams.

The strangest things are there for me,
Both things to eat and things to see,
And many frightening sights abroad
Till morning in the land of Nod.

Try as I like to find the way,
I never can get back by day,
Nor can remember plain and clear
The curious music that I hear.

MY SHADOW
by Robert Louis Stevenson

I have a little shadow that goes in and out with
        me,
And what can be the use of him is more than I
        can see.
He is very, very like me from the heels up to the
        head;
And I can see him jump before me, when I jump
        into my bed.

The funniest thing about him is the way he likes
        to grow—
Not at all like proper children, which is always
        very slow;
For he sometimes shoots up taller, like an india-
        rubber-ball,
And he sometimes gets so little that there's none
        of him at all.

He hasn't got a notion of how children ought be
        play,
And can only make a fool of me in every sort of
        way.
He stays so close beside me, he's a coward you
        can see;
I'd think shame to stick to nursie as that shadow
        sticks to me!

One morning, very early, before the sun came up,
I rose and found the shining dew on every butter-
        cup;

But my lazy little shadow, like an arrant sleepy-
  head,
Had stayed at home behind me and was fast
  asleep in bed.

MY LITTLE BROTHER
by Mary Lundie Duncan

Little brother, darling boy
    You are very dear to me!
I am happy—full of joy,
    When your smiling face I see.

How I wish that you could speak,
    And could know the words I say!
Pretty stories I would seek
    To amuse you every day,—

All about the honey-bees,
    Flying past us in the sun;
Birds that sing among the trees,
    Lambs that in the meadows run.

Shake your rattle—here it is—
    Listen to its merry noise;
And, when you are tired of this,
    I will bring you other toys.

MY LITTLE SISTER

I have a little sister,
    She is only two years old;
But to us at home, who love her,
    She is worth her weight in gold.

We often play together;
    And I begin to find,
That to make my sister happy,
    I must be very kind;

And always very gentle
    When we run about and play,
Nor ever take her playthings
    Or little toys away.

I must not vex or tease her,
    Nor ever angry be
With the darling little sister
    That God has given to me.

PLAYGROUNDS
by Laurence Alma-Tadema

In summer I am very glad
    We children are so small,
For we can see a thousand things
    That men can't see at all.

They don't know much about the moss
    And all the stones they pass:
They never lie and play among
    The forests in the grass:

They walk about a long way off;
    And, when we're at the sea,
Let father stoop as best he can
    He can't find things like me.

But, when the snow is on the ground
    And all the puddles freeze,
I wish that I were very tall,
    High up above the trees.

THE TEAPOT DRAGON
by Rupert Sargent Holland

There's a dragon on our teapot,
    With a long and crinkly tail,
His claws are like a pincer-bug,
    His wings are like a sail;

His tongue is always sticking out,
    And so I used to think
He must be very hungry, or
    He wanted tea to drink.

But once when Mother wasn't round
    I dipped my fingers in,
And when I pulled them out I found
    I'd blistered all the skin.

Now when I see the dragon crawl
    Around our china pot,
I know he's burned his tongue because
    The water is so hot.

"ONE, TWO, THREE"
by H. C. Bunner

It was an old, old, old lady
    And a boy that was half-past three,
And the way that they played together
    Was beautiful to see.

She couldn't go romping and jumping,
    And the boy, no more could he;
For he was a thin little fellow,
    With a thin little twisted knee.

They sat in the yellow sunlight,
    Out under the maple tree,
And the game that they played I'll tell you,
    Just as it was told to me.

It was hide-and-seek they were playing,
    Though you'd never had known it to be—
With an old, old, old lady
    And a boy with a twisted knee.

They boy would bend his face down
    On his little sound right knee,
And he guessed where she was hiding
    In guesses One, Two, Three.

"You are in the china closet!"
    He would cry, and laugh with glee—
It wasn't the china closet,
    But he still has Two and Three.

"You are up in papa's big bedroom,
    In the chest with the queer old key,"
And she said: "You are warm and warmer;
    But you are not quite right," said she.

"It can't be the little cupboard
    Where mamma's things used to be—
So it must be in the clothes press, Gran-ma
    And he found her with his Three.

Then she covered her face with her fingers,
    That were wrinkled and white and wee,
And she guessed where the boy was hiding,
    With a One and a Two and a Three.

And they never had stirred from their places
    Right under the maple tree—
This old, old, old, old lady
    And the boy with the lame little knee—
This dear, dear, dear old lady
    And the boy who was half-past three.

LITTLE ORPHANT ANNIE
by *James Whitcomb Riley*

Little Orphant Annie's come to our
    house to stay,
An' wash the cups and saucers up, an'
    brush the crumbs away,
An' shoo the chickens off the porch,
    an' dust the hearth, an' sweep,
An' make the fire, an' bake the bread,
    an' earn her board-an'-keep;
An' all us other children, when the
    supper things is done,
We set around the kitchen fire an' has
    the mostest fun
A-list'nin' to the witch-tales 'at Annie
    tells about,
An' the Gobble-uns 'at gits you
    Ef you
        Don't
            Watch
              Out!

Wunst they was a little boy wouldn't
    say his prayers,—
An' when he went to bed at night,
    away up-stairs,
His Mammy heerd him holler, an' his
    Daddy heerd him bawl,
An' when they turn't the kivvers
    down, he wazn't there at all!
An' they seeked him in the rafter-
    room, an' cubby-hole, an' press,

An' seeked him up the chimbly-flue,
    an' ever'wheres, I guess;
But all they ever found wuz thist his
    pants an' round-about:—
An' the Gobble-uns 'll git you
    Ef you
        Don't
            Watch
                Out!

An' one time a little girl 'ud allus
    laugh and grin,
An' make fun of ever'one, an' all her
    blood-an'-kin;
An' wunst, when they wuz "company,"
    an' ole folks wuz there,
She mocked 'em an' shocked 'em, an'
    said she didn't care!
An' thist as she kicked her heels, an'
    turn't to run an' hide,
They wuz two great big Black Things
    a-standin' by her side,
An' they snatched her through the
    ceilin' 'fore she knowed what
    she's about!
An' the Gobble-uns 'll git you
    Ef you
        Don't
            Watch
                Out!

An' little Orphant Annie says, when
the blaze is blue,
An' the lamp wick sputters, an' the
wind goes *woo-oo!*
An' you hear the crickets quit, an'
the moon is gray,
An' the lightnin'-bugs in dew is all
squenched away,—
You better mind yer parunts, an' yer
teachers fond an' dear,
An' churish them 'at loves you, an'
dry the orphant's tear,
An' he'p the pore an' needy ones 'at
clusters all about,
Er the Goble-uns 'll git you
    Ef you
        Don't
            Watch
                Out!

THE HAPPY PIPER
by William Blake

Piping down the valleys wild,
    Piping songs of pleasant glee,
On a cloud I saw a child,
    And he laughing said to me:

"Pipe a song about a Lamb!"
    So I piped with merry cheer.
"Piper, pipe that song again;"
    So I piped: he wept to hear.

"Drop thy pipe, thy happy pipe;
    Sing thy songs of happy cheer!"
So I sang the same again,
    While he wept with joy to hear.

"Piper, sit thee down and write
    In a book that all may read."
So he vanish'd from my sight,
    And I pluck'd a hollow reed,

And I made a rural pen,
    And I stain'd the water clear,
And I wrote my happy songs
    Every child may joy to hear.

THE LAND OF THE STORY-BOOKS
by Robert Louis Stevenson

At evening when the lamp is lit,
Around the fire my parents sit;
They sit at home and talk and sing,
And do not play at anything.

Now, with my little gun, I crawl
All in the dark along the wall,
And follow round the forest track
Away behind the sofa back.

There, in the night, where none can spy,
All in my hunter's camp I lie,
And play at books that I have read
Till it is time to go to bed.

These are the hills, these are the woods,
These are my starry solitudes;
And there the river by whose brink
The roaring lions come to drink.

I see the others far away
As if in firelit camp they lay,
And I, like to an Indian scout,
Around their party prowled about.

So, when my nurse comes in for me,
Home I return across the sea,
And go to bed with backward looks
At my dear land of Story-books.

THE LAND OF COUNTERPANE
by Robert Louis Stevenson

When I was sick and lay a-bed
I had two pillows at my head,
And all my toys beside me lay
To keep me happy all the day.

And sometimes for an hour or so
I watched my leaden soldiers go,
With different uniforms and drills,
Among the bed-clothes, through the hills;

And sometimes sent my ships in fleets
All up and down among the sheets;
Or brought my trees and houses out,
And planted cities all about.

I was the giant great and still
That sits upon the pillow-hill,
And sees before him, dale and plain,
The pleasant land of counterpane.

THE BLUE BOY IN LONDON
by *William Brighty Rands*

All in the morning early
    The Little Boy in Blue
(The grass with rain is pearly)
    Has thought of something new.

He saddled dear old Dobbin;
    He had but half a crown;
And jogging, cantering, bobbing,
    He came to London town.

The sheep were in the meadows,
    The cows were in the corn,
Beneath the city shadow
    As last he stood forlorn.

He stood beneath Bow steeple,
    That is in London town;
And tried to count the people
    As they went up and down.

Oh! there was not a daisy
    And not a buttercup;
The air was thick and hazy,
    And Blue Boy gave it up.

The houses, next, in London,
    He thought that he would count;
But still the sum was undone,
    So great was the amount.

He could not think of robbing—
    He had but half a crown;
And so he mounted Dobbin,
    And rode back from the town.

The sheep were in the meadows,
    And the cows were in the corn;
Amid the evening shadows
    He stood where he was born.

ONE AND ONE
by Mary Mapes Dodge

Two little girls are better than one,
Two little boys can double the fun,
Two little birds can build a fine nest,
Two little arms can love mother best.
Two little ponies must go to a span;
Two little pockets has my little man;
Two little eyes to open and close,
Two little ears and one little nose,
Two little elbows, dimpled and sweet,
Two little shoes on two little feet,
Two little lips and one little chin,
Two little cheeks with a rose shut in;
Two little shoulders, chubby and strong,
Two little legs running all day long.
Two little prayers does my darling say,
Twice does he kneel by my side each day,
Two little folded hands, soft and brown,
Two little eyelids cast meekly down,
And two little angels guard him in bed,
"One at the foot, and one at the head."

THE ARROW AND THE SONG
by Henry Wordsworth Longfellow

I shot an arrow into the air,
It fell to earth, I knew not where;
For, so swiftly it flew, the sight
Could not follow it in its flight.

I breathed a song into the air,
It fell to earth, I knew not where;
For who has sight so keen and strong,
That it can follow the flight of song?

Long, long afterward, in an oak
I found the arrow, still unbroke;
And the song, from beginning to end,
I found again in the heart of a friend.

THE NIGHT HAS A THOUSAND EYES
by Francis William Bourdillon

The night has a thousand eyes,
    And the day but one;
Yet the light of the bright world dies
    With the dying sun.

The mind has a thousand eyes,
    And the heart but one;
Yet the light of a whole life dies
    When love is done.

WHEN I GROW UP
by Rupert Sargent Holland

When I grow up I mean to go
Where all the biggest rivers flow,
And take a ship and sail around
The Seven Seas until I've found
Robinson Crusoe's famous isle,
And there I'll land and stay a while,
And see how it would feel to be
Lord of an island in the sea.

When I grow up I mean to rove
Through orange and palmetto grove,
To drive a sledge across the snow
Where great explorers like to go,
To hunt to treasures hid of old
By buccaneers and pirates bold,
And see if somewhere there may be
A mountain no one's climbed but me.

When I grow up I mean to do
The things I've always wanted to;
I don't see why grown people stay
At home, when they could be away.

Index of First Lines